Phui Yee

HAVE COURAGE: LIVE YOUR PASSION

One Mother's Message to Her Daughter

AUSTIN MACAULEY PUBLISHERS™

LONDON • CAMBRIDGE • NEW YORK • SHARJAH

A CIP catalogue record for this title is available from the British Library.

ISBN 978-1-78823-616-4 (Paperback)
ISBN 978-1-78823-617-1 (E-Book)
www.austinmacauley.com

First Published (2019)
Austin Macauley Publishers Ltd.
25 Canada Square
Canary Wharf
London
E14 5LQ

To my beautiful daughter, Hannah

CONTENTS

Dear Hannah,

This book has been written specially for you. It is my way of saying I love you and that you are the most important person in my life. I am so honoured to be your mum and I want to thank you for choosing to share your life with me.

Every day, I notice that you are growing up and changing as part of your journey in finding yourself and creating your life. I would love to protect you for as long as I can, in fact, I would love to be able to wrap you in cotton wool to make sure no harm can ever come to you. But if I did, that would be unhealthy. It would also be unnatural; and if I protected you this way, I would be denying you your freedom and your opportunity to have the biggest and most amazing adventure possible in time and space. In fact, I would be denying you the only reason you came to this world: to live your life.

As a mother, my basic instinct is to love you, protect you and provide for you. It is my job to make sure that you do the 'right' things according to my own limited knowledge of what is right and wrong. I know I am over-protective at times, and I know you hate it when I won't even let you walk down to the local shop on your own, but it is my belief about how to be a good mum that firmly guides this decision.

I have so many things I want to share with you, but I want to be careful not to damage our relationship in the process. I have this vision of me being the 'swag mum', where you and I are best friends, and you can talk to me about anything and everything. We go travelling together and do lots of cool things together. I want to be around for you when you need me, and I want to be the first person you call when you are in trouble, knowing you can talk to me without fear or judgement.

You are fourteen, going on fifteen, and I realise it's time for me to share with you what I have learned in my life. I'm not writing this to tell you how great or clever I am; in fact, it is quite the opposite. I would like to share with you all the mistakes I have made in my life, lessons I have learned the hard way and all the chaos I have created over the past thirty years in the hope that my adventure will help to guide you on your journey to creating an amazing and fulfilling life for yourself.

You are my beautiful hero and always will be. With deepest love from my heart,

Mummy

INTRODUCTION

THE SEED OF the idea for this book was probably planted about two years ago. It came out of the frustration I felt when I found myself lost for words and couldn't express my thoughts to my daughter, Hannah. It was when I discovered that I didn't know how to teach her what I wanted her to know or show her what I wanted her to see or even comfort her in a meaningful way that this book began to be formed in my mind. There are times in life when things need to be said, wisdom passed on and laughter shared, but I was so caught up in my own anxiety, fear, worry and anger that I let these moments where I could share my experience slip through my fingers. I only realised that I had missed these precious moments when I had finally calmed down after the event. Each time, I wished I could turn back the clock and do things differently, seize the moment and make it count.

When she was five, Hannah came home from school feeling upset, and all I could do was give her a cuddle and tell her everything was going to be all right. But that wasn't good enough! I wanted to tell her that God and the Universe are on her side and that she needed to change her thought patterns, and expect and be ready to receive. But I couldn't. It wasn't the right moment, and it wasn't a simple lesson for me to pass on in that moment. I knew that Hannah needed to understand why I was saying what I was saying. Otherwise, she might misunderstand my true meaning and feel more confused and distressed.

I am not an articulate person. I call a spade, a spade. Well, what else can you call a spade? As a result, I tend to hold back and end up regretting not saying what I should say 'in the moment'. When the moment has passed and the dust has settled, sentence after sentence of wisdom come into my mind but by then, it is too late.

My relationship with my daughter is a typical mother and daughter one. We laugh together, have our fair share of arguments and debates, express anger and even rudeness at times, but most of all, our strongest emotion is love. This book is my attempt to communicate and pass on what I know about life to my beautiful daughter, Hannah. I do not want her to grow up not understanding the power she has or have to go through what I have been through in my life. I am sure she will still live her life her way, embarking on all the adventures the journey of life throws at her. I hope this book will provide her with the tools and techniques she needs to get her through all the challenges she encounters on her journey.

I am sure she will fall down many times as she lives her life, but I hope with the knowledge contained in this book, she will be able to get back on her feet faster and get stronger as she continues on her way. I also hope this book will provide her with a compass when she is lost and strength when she experiences challenging times.

During my time working in social housing as a Building Surveyor in the UK, I have undertaken quite a few home visits as part of my job. During these visits, I meet many tenants. Some tenants are two-parent families, some single parent families, some vulnerable elderly men and women and some are young adults in sheltered housing.

In every county, there are areas described as 'council housing' that many people shy away from living in if they can. These areas have a reputation for high levels of crime rates, badly-behaved children, poorly-performing schools, dog fouling and anything else undesirable.

Well, that might have been the case 50 years ago, but I believe most of these places have improved considerably since then. Most of the residents have changed too. Those naughty boys and girls are now in their fifties and sixties, and new generations have moved in. However, perceptions, once formed are difficult to change. This is one of the issues we will look at in this book.

One of the problems I have encountered in these council housing areas is that there are still a few small pockets of tenants and residents whose expectations of life are what they were when they were children, and they are passing those same beliefs on to their children and grandchildren. As a result, I have met many children and young adults who are lost and who live under the illusion that living on benefits is the only way of life they can expect. They spend their whole life trying to get away from their disjointed family environments, get free housing from the local government and rely on benefits for their living expenses. Most of these children are never shown a different way because their parents don't know another way. Even their grandparents don't know another way.

On one visit, I was working as the Disabled Adaptation Grant Officer for a local authority and I met a family where three generations were sitting at home every day, living on benefits. The client I went to see was the father of five children: the eldest (a boy) was 18 and the youngest (a girl) was around six. The client was probably in his fifties and he was ill. I was there to look at the possibility of helping him get a grant so he could to adapt his property to suit his needs.

Part of my job was to look at my client's financial situation to see if he qualified for a grant. In the process of completing the financial forms, the client listed all the benefits he claimed. His total income from benefits was over £25,000 a year. He then turned around and said to me, "Is there any other benefits that you know that I can claim? Have I missed anything else that is available?" I was dismayed and shocked and I didn't know how to respond.

He saw me looking at his children and he said, "None of my children have a job and I have never worked. My parents and siblings have never worked. We all live on benefits—all three generations." I walked away from that household feeling faint—I thought it was a joke. The children did not know anything else. Their parents, grandparents, aunts and uncles were their role models. Each of their role models was showing them how to live a wasted life! Given half a chance, the children could have decent jobs. Some could be future prime ministers, scientists, entrepreneurs or teachers. These children went to school but they had no motivation to succeed. As the Chinese say: "Anything that touches vermillion will be stained red; anything that touches ink will be dyed black." (In other words, one's morals are influenced by the company one keeps). Sadly, this situation is not an isolated example.

About three years ago, I met a girl who had attempted suicide. She was being cared for at one of the sheltered homes where I worked. She was living with a foster carer because her mother was in prison and her father left them when she was ten. She was 16 when I met her and couldn't see a future for herself.

While running a Kitchen Replacement Programme for a housing association, I walked into a property where young children were living in a home that had faeces in the bathtub and on the living room floor. The house stank. The three year old boy in the family looked unwell and the mother was stressed. What will happen to this little boy? There are children who live in homes full of junk because one of their parents is a hoarder. There are many children who do not have parents at all or who have been kicked out by their parents. There are many more disturbing situations that I can tell you about but I won't go on. I wonder what the future will hold for these children, young adults and families.

I am hoping this book will be able to reach out to people in these situations. I hope I can show them a different way. I sincerely hope I can help these children and young adults harness the power within them to create a life that is fulfilling and exciting. I know I won't be able to reach out to every single one of them, but if I can only help a handful, there will be hope for the rest.

It is my goal to be an inspiration to those who are less fortunate and to people who are going through challenges in their lives. I hope this book will bring courage, love and hope to those who need it so they can understand the power that is within each one of us. It is my heartfelt desire that this book will plant the seed of faith that is there for everyone who asks and everyone who believes in it. Most of all, I want to tell you not to give up on your life and never give in to the challenges you face. Have courage and embrace love. Live with passion and fuel your everyday life with your aspirations. To help set you on your way, I would like to share my own passions and aspirations.

1) My dream since childhood has been to open orphanages around the world that can give children a loving home where they feel special and can have a fulfilling life, no matter where they started.

2) It is my ambition to open homeless shelters around the world.

3) I want to help those who are willing to help themselves. I want to offer food and warmth, but I want to go further than this by helping them to start all over again.

4) I want to reach out to schools and education establishments so I can share the message of this book with children and young adults.

5) I believe that if I can get my message to children and young adults they will have a better chance of living a fulfilling and prosperous life. This will help to create a prosperous and successful world.

6) I would like to take my message to Malaysia, my home country, so I can help my fellow Malaysians to improve their lives, be successful and prosper so they can create and lead more fulfilled

lives. It is my way of giving back to the country I love and that I grew up in.

7) My other passion is food. I love food, and I enjoy eating. One of my aspirations is to open a restaurant that serves my favourite foods and drinks. I am constantly amazed by the talent of chefs around the world. I am fascinated by the diversity of cooking styles from different countries, even from different villages in many regions. I have a big collection of cookbooks, and they are often my bedtime reading when I am not reading a self- improvement book.

8) Travelling is another of my passions. Food and travel go hand in hand in my opinion. I remember when I was at college, living in Kuala Lumpur, I woke up one morning and decided to take a coach to Malacca, a historic city in Malaysia so I could spend the weekend exploring it. I took a small backpack and off I went. It was such a good feeling to do what I love and to be free to do it spontaneously. Life lived in freedom is magical.

9) I want to learn to play the piano (I have wanted to do this since I was eight years old!). I have now started piano lessons and at the time of writing, I will be having my eighth lesson this week!

10) It is my goal to provide the best for Hannah in every aspect of her life. Hannah is my inspiration, my passion, my reason to get up every morning and do what I do.

What is your passion, and what are your aspirations? Do you have a bucket list or wish list of what you dream of doing and achieving with your life? If not? Then write one now and keep adding to it as you learn about new passions and dreams.

HOW THIS BOOK IS ORGANISED

Part One

Part One of this book introduces you to the fundamental rules and theories behind our thinking, the way our minds work, the Universe and God. Think of it as week one of your Reception Year at school. It is important that you read this book with an open mind and that you are ready to consider new concepts, even though they may sound ridiculous to you at first.

I have used the word God in a few parts of this book because I feel it is time we start to see the true meaning of the word after thousands of years of misleading information and images all portrayed in the name of God. The word God conjures up a mixture of emotions and images for many of us so I was tempted to substitute it for the phrase, 'the Universe'. But I decided not to do this because I want to teach Hannah to have courage, believe in the truth and to make decision based on her own ideas. If I choose to remove the word 'God' or substitute it with 'the Universe', I might as well give up writing this book now.

'God' is not a bad word just as 'money' is not an evil entity. It is the meaning we give to these words that has skewed the true value of the word. I also believe that although God reigns over the Universe, God does not equal the Universe. God does not belong to any religion. God exists outside of religion. However, religion cannot exist without God. Therefore, in this book, I am talking about God as a standalone entity not within the context of any religion.

I hope by the end of this book, you will have some new healthy beliefs and that you will be able to conjure up positive emotions around the words 'God' and 'money' because a clear understanding of these two words will open you to the source of prosperity in your life.

"Life is really simple, but we insist on making it complicated."

CONFUCIUS

Part Two

Part Two of the book is more practical. After learning the theories and fundamental rules of how to live a life of passion in Part One, I apply these rules to real life situations in Part Two. I will give examples, share tools and describe techniques that will help you take your first steps towards creating the life of your dreams. This is where you must take action if you want to see changes in your life.

"No one saves us but ourselves. No one can and no one may. We ourselves must walk the path."

BUDDHA

Of course, this book is written with my 14-year-old daughter in mind. I am not writing it to gain fame or fortune but because of the desire to share with my daughter the lessons I have learnt, the adventures I have had and the amazing people I have met along the way.

I do not know how I will be remembered when I pass over, especially by my precious daughter. I am just a mother who, like every other mother, wants the best for her daughter, and I hope this book will deliver that message loud and clear.

I have written this book for those who are new to the concepts I discuss here, so if you are more familiar with what I am saying, please feel free to pick the tools and techniques that work for you. In due course, you will be able to develop tools that resonate with you more deeply than those I describe here. Read more books so you can expand your knowledge about similar subjects or other ideas that interest you. To help you, I have created a list of recommended books and authors for your reference.

Let's begin our journey.

"It does not matter how slowly you go as long as you do not stop."

CONFUCIUS

PART ONE

CHAPTER ONE
You Are Talented and Special For a Reason
天 生 我 才 必 有 用

YOU ARE SPECIAL. Everyone is special—and unique. No two people that have lived on this planet have ever been the same, not even twins. Each and every one of us is a unique individual and part of what makes us unique is our very own special talents. They are your gifts. You may not know what your special talents are right now, but there is a reason why you have been born with your unique and special blend of the ones you have.

When a baby is born, everyone looks at the baby adoringly. They smile and feel joy when they look at him/her. The baby is not expected to do anything except stay alive, eat and sleep. As long as the baby does these three amazing things, everyone is happy. However, expectations start to change as the baby grows. There are milestones the baby is expected to achieve as she grows older. She is expected to make cute babbling noises before mastering her first syllables. She is expected to crawl or, at least, shuffle around by a certain age, and she is expected to take her first step by the time she is twelve months old.

Unlike 'normal' toddlers, Hannah was not walking by the time she was one year old. Mama (my mother) watched her every move. Every day, she tried to train Hannah to take her first steps. Mama was worried and said things like 'lazy girl' to Hannah for not making the effort to take her first steps. When Hannah finally decided to take her first steps on Southsea seafront on a cold winter's afternoon, Mama was overjoyed! At last, her beautiful granddaughter was walking at 13 months, and most importantly, Mama was there to witness that priceless moment.

Hannah was now a 'good girl' instead of a 'lazy girl'. Mama loved Hannah dearly, and she would never hurt her in any way. Mama calling Hannah a 'lazy girl' was simply a reflection of the way she was conditioned to cope with this particular event in her life. Mama did not mean to be unkind. It was more of a 'reverse psychology' technique she was using: tell Hannah she's lazy and, perhaps, she'll try harder.

The truth is that we are all expected to achieve certain things or learn particular skills at specific ages. But this means we unconsciously put ourselves in a box because of the expectations of society, family, peers, and the world—even if it is done with the best of intentions. As a result, most of us never have the opportunity to find out who we really are. We're so busy being pushed from one milestone to another and doing what everyone else expects us to do that we never have time to decide what it is that we truly want to do. If you cannot meet a particular challenge or master a required skill, you get labelled or type-cast as 'un-creative', 'not technical' or maybe even 'lazy'. Why can't people just take us as we are?

'Labelling' or 'type-casting' has been going on for thousands of years but these days, instead of type-casting people by their social status, we type-cast people by their achievements. If you can't meet a particular milestones or expectation or if you can't do certain things, it's assumed that you must be ill, or there must be something wrong with you. If you don't achieve your grades at school, there is no hope for you, and you'll end up being a road sweeper.

In recent years, scientists have revealed that human beings only use up to ten per cent of their brain. Perhaps in years to come, spiritual masters or scientists may be able to show us how to use more than ten per cent, but for now let's work with that figure. What if those of us who find it difficult to learn certain skills actually do not know how to use our brains like most people? What if I am only able to use three per cent of my brain? It may mean I am not receptive to conventional teaching styles, but I am sure I will be able to learn in a different way, or there may be some beliefs or blocks that are preventing me from learning.

When I was young, I found learning to read and write difficult because my brain functions differently. I couldn't sit still for more than ten minutes at a time. So what? Give me a chance. Give your children a chance; Give your co-workers a chance. Once the brain accepts the label of 'learning disabled', we will potentially become that label for the rest of our lives. Our brain will do whatever it takes to ensure the statement is true. It becomes a self-fulfilling prophecy. I have seen it many times in my workplace, as well as from those who attend my seminars.

We are constantly measuring our lives and progress against the achievements of others to the point where we forget to recognise the talents we do have. We focus so much on comparing ourselves that we lose sight of our own special gifts and our own dreams. It is time to put away your measuring tape today and see yourself for who you really are. Whoever you think you are, please remember this:

- You are not who others say you are, so don't accept any labels you are given by others.
- You are not what you posted on Facebook.
- You are not a tweet or your profile on social media accounts.
- You are not your job or your education.
- You are not the things you own or the things you do.
- You are not just a daughter, mother, father, husband, wife, sister, brother, friend or a neighbour.

❈ *My Story*

It all started on my first day at kindergarten. I don't remember anything about what I did on that day, or what I learnt in my lessons, but I clearly remember my new classmates giggling and whispering to each other when I was introduced to the class by my teacher. It was my first day at a new school after moving to Kuantan because of my dad's job. When I walked into the classroom with Mama, the teacher made a comment about my appearance. I was tall for a seven year-old, and I was broad too. My cousins called me 'Fei Mui' in Chinese, which means 'fat girl' and there was nothing I could do to make them stop. To them, it was an innocent joke—they thought I should be open-minded and accept their label with joy. When I was upset, Mama said that I was narrow-minded, and it was silly of me to cry. It may be silly to others, but it still hurt me every time I heard them say it.

I have been labelled 'fat girl' for as long as I can remember, and now my brain accepts this statement as a fact. As you have probably guessed, I have never been slim in my life despite going on many diets and even taking medication. I am fat. My New Year's resolution for the past thirty years has been to lose three stones in weight. Has it ever happened? Yes, it did for a few years, but I put the pounds back on as soon as I went back to believing I was a fat girl again. It doesn't matter what or how other people perceive me, I see myself as fat, unattractive and ugly because over the years, my brain has been conditioned to believe the judgement made by my family and friends: I am fat and, therefore, I am ugly.

When I was in Malaysia, whenever I bumped into friends or family, the first thing anyone said to me was "Hi, Sam! You have put on weight!" It was very rare that my friends would say, "Hi, Sam! You have lost weight!" How did I feel about this? I felt sad, angry, annoyed and frustrated. I constantly had the urge to reach out and strangle the person standing in front of me who, incidentally, always had a big smile on his or her face. So instead of letting off steam, I had to be polite, hold in my anger and smile and agree with them. The moment I said "Yes, I know", another signal was sent to my brain confirming the thought, *I am fat*. The worse was that the thought was heightened by being emotionally charged by my rage. That's why my thought started to change into a belief.

When you accept the names or labels given to you by your peers, family, friends, colleagues and neighbours, you gradually become conditioned to believe it is true, whether that statement serves you or not. But you are not defined by others. You are born with special gifts and talents, and you are here for a reason. You are special—one in a billion—so never give your power away to others. Next, let's begin to explore your gifts and discover why you have been given your own special talents.

CHAPTER TWO
Let's Be Magnificent

NOW THAT YOU have discovered that you are special, let's not stop there, and let's make you magnificent and outstanding! What was your first thought when you read that sentence?

Did you think?

- *Fantastic! I'm inspired by the thought that I can be magnificent and outstanding.*
- *I'm so excited!*
- *That's amazing! I can now see myself being magnificent.*

Or did you think?

- *Who, me? Make me magnificent? In your dreams!*
- *You must be kidding!*
- *Outstanding? You must be kidding!*
- *You think I'm special? You must be high on something!*

There is no right or wrong reaction to that opening sentence, but your response will tell you something important. It will give you an insight into your beliefs. Beliefs are filters through which we each see the world. Your beliefs form a system of 'rules' that you have accepted as true. However, most of the time, they have no bearing on reality because your beliefs are not objective.

Our personal belief system has been formed over time by a combination of different sources of information, from our culture to our social conditioning. Many of our beliefs are modelled from listening to parents, family, friends, peers, teachers and any other data we have been subjected to since birth. Each one of us has a different set of beliefs based on our experience. Together, our beliefs provide us with a survival kit that allows us to get through our lives day by day so we can maximise our pleasure and minimise our pain.

There are thousands of rules that go to make up a complete belief system. Most of these rules are positive and extremely valuable. In fact it isn't so much that there are bad rules underpinning a belief system; it's more that those rules can become restrictive and out of date. As children, we learnt from our parents, teachers and guardians to make sure we stayed safe. But as we grew up, that focus on safety is what stops us from taking calculated risks, taking on challenges and growing. As our needs, desires and dreams change, our old beliefs no longer serve us. But the problem only comes up when we stop being aware that it is a rule or a belief that is affecting our choices, responses and actions.

Five years ago, I had never heard of beliefs, so I had no way to identify them or change them. You have to be able to see something before you can change it, after all, you will find it difficult to clean your house if you can't see the mess, dust and dirt all around you. In the same way, I couldn't see the beliefs that were holding me back. Here are some examples of negative beliefs you may have (I shared quite a few of these):

I am not good enough because…

- Life is stressful and challenging.
- I will never have enough money.
- No one will ever love me for who I am.
- I am fat and ugly.
- I am not good at netball, hockey, swimming, etc.
- Chief Executives have to be nasty, and they live in cloud cuckoo land.
- Rich people are stingy.
- I am stuck in a rut, and nothing can get me out of this situation.
- I am bad with money.
- I am not clever like other girls/boys/men/woman, etc.
- I cannot afford that car, house, handbag, shoes, etc.
- I will never be an all A-grade student.
- Public speaking is terrifying!
- Accepting gifts—or anything else that is free—means you are greedy.

With so much dirt in my head, no wonder I was leading such a mediocre life! In the culture I grew up, when something bad happened to someone or when things didn't go their way, people would say things like: "It wasn't meant to be", "It is fate!" or "It is part of your path to enlightenment". Below are some examples of things I have heard people say when things don't go well for them:

"I was robbed."

It is your fate. According to your birth date and time, you were meant to be robbed this year. Things will be good from now on.

"My business failed."

Oh, yes. It is your path and prediction for this year. Do not start another business until you are 45, you will not have any luck in business until then. You will fail at everything until you are 45!

"I was suspended from work due to alleged fraud."

Yes, this year you have an evil spirit around you that will cause financial chaos in your life and affect your relationship with your boss and colleagues. Don't worry! Everything will be fine next year. Ask your mum to beat the evil spirit at the temple, and everything will be fine.

"I married the wrong man" (or "I married a man who abused me regularly.")

This is your fate. This is due to a debt you needed to repay from a previous life.

When something good happens, everyone says the opposite: "It is meant to be", "It is your destiny to experience success, wealth and blessings". If good things happened, it was put down to someone having done good deeds in a previous life. If bad things happened, it was seen as a punishment for what we did in a previous life. If someone did something very bad, it was thought that they would be reincarnated as pigs!

As you can see, the Chinese culture is very superstitious! Everything that happened was attributed to events in a previous life, unpaid cosmic debts or the time or date when someone was born, but it was never the individual's fault. All power was handed over without a quibble or a qualm to the great unknown force of destiny. If I had known back then what I know now, I would never have accepted these predictions and superstitions as reality. Today, I use my knowledge to improve my life and take whatever action is necessary for me to walk my own path and hold supportive beliefs.

I now question superstitious statements and aim to take each with a pinch of salt! Although, to tell you the truth, I do believe these predictions a little, but now I don't believe them unquestioningly. I find the old predictions and stories fascinating. Most of them are based on superstitions or are part of a mythology that was passed down through generations. When I was small, I used to feel scared and worried by them, but now, I enjoy recalling the time I spent with my grandma when she would tell me the stories as I helped her to prepare the feed for the chickens, turkeys and geese in our backyard. Let me share a few of the superstitions I grew up with so you can see how bizarre and funny some of them are.

- Don't go near flowers or plants after dark as you may disturb the flower spirits who come out at night to feed. If you upset the spirits, they will take you away with them and you'll never be seen again.

- When you hear dogs barking at night, it means there are ghosts or spirits out playing. Stay at home when that happens. (Funnily enough, the dogs in my village barked every night so I never dared go out after dark. But then, that was the point: to keep me safe indoors!)

- In Chinese culture, when someone passes away, the funeral ceremony goes on for three nights. During this time, the coffin is displayed at the front of the home of the deceased. All night, prayers are led by Buddhist funeral directors (Nam Mo Lo, in Chinese). During each night, family members take it in turn to watch over the coffin to make sure no black cats come near it (Yes, black cats are the most feared animal where dead bodies are concerned). The Chinese believe that if a black cat manages to jump on or over the coffin, the soul of the deceased will follow the black cat instead of going to heaven!

- As children, we were told to clear our plates or bowls at every meal. Not a single grain of rice could be left; otherwise, we would marry someone with lots of spots or scars on their face, or in other words, someone ugly.

- Never clip your nails at night because if you accidentally cut yourself you will bleed uncontrollably (That nail clipper was clearly lethal!).

- Sit still at the dinner table or you will be poor when you grow up.

- If you tell lies, the King of Hell will cut off your tongue when you die (Presumably you would also go to hell for telling lies).

- If you do not respect and look after your own parents, when you are old your children will not respect and look after you. Many Chinese people take this to heart because no one wants to be abandoned by their children when they are old and vulnerable.

All the above formed part of the Chinese belief system. It affects Chinese people from the day they are born because they are conditioned to believe it by their parents, friends, peers and general social environment. These beliefs are rooted in my ancestry, not just my generation or the previous generations. Everyone who grows up in this culture accepts these ideas as true and few challenge the authenticity of these beliefs. But even if they did, I don't think they would get very far. The main problem is that, just like me, most are not aware of how these beliefs or rules affect their lives. Even more importantly, as I discovered, it was very hard for me to consciously change my beliefs because these ideas are ingrained in my psyche. That's why many of us are slaves to our own personal belief system.

"It all depends on how we look at things, and not how they are in themselves."

CARL JUNG

❈ *My Story*

I was born in a small village in Malaysia called Kampong Timah. My grandparents had fled from China during World War II along with their six children. My dad was their second son and the fourth child in the family. Life was very difficult, and my grandma had to give away her second daughter (my second aunt) to a family in the next village as a young bride. She was just eight years old at the time. My aunt (Yi Gu Ma) had to take care of her new husband and look after her in-laws so she was a servant to everyone in the household. Yi Gu Ma was bitter all her life, and we sadly lost her to cancer in 2014.

In Kampung Timah, most villagers are Chinese and practise Buddhism. They hold many common beliefs. Here are just a few of them. Many of these beliefs would have been shared by Yi Gu Ma.

- Life is hard.
- Life is unfair.
- We are poor, because we live in a village.
- Only rich people live in the city.
- Boys are superior to and more important than girls.
- Girls are meant to be housewives so they don't need any education.
- Handsome men and pretty women are unfaithful.
- Rich men are unfaithful.

By holding on to these beliefs, our village has been prevented from changing for the past 50 years. Even today, people in the village still believe these ideas. Like the relatives who went before them, they live in the same houses, run the same businesses and carry out the same rituals every day.

I am the eldest child in my family, but my grandparents were not pleased when I was born because they believed that girls are not worthwhile. Girls are seen as a poor investment. The most ridiculous part is that Mama got the blame! It was Mama's fault that I was born a girl. My grandma has been unkind to Mama ever since I was born. My two uncles' first-born children were sons so their wives were elevated to a higher position in the family over Mama. According to my grandma, my two aunties can't do a thing wrong.

I was brought up to believe that I wasn't good enough. I believed that to earn the approval of my parents and grandparents, I needed to be a boy. That, of course, was impossible for me to achieve because I couldn't transform myself from a girl to a boy. As a result, I spent my whole life trying to earn my family's approval, but my needs were rarely considered. I was always at the bottom of the pile because I was a girl. Here is a sample of the beliefs I held when I was growing up:

- I will never be good enough because I am a girl.
- I cannot be a man, but I can act like a man.
- I do not want to depend on men all my life.
- I will have to struggle all my life.
- I can't have it all.

- Handsome men and rich men are unfaithful so I will have to marry someone who is not as good looking as me so that he will not leave me for someone else.
- My mission is to please everyone, to make sure my family approve of what I do and that I do what they want me to do.
- I must never say 'No'.
- My family is poor.
- It is my duty to provide for my family—parents, brothers and sister. They come first.

These beliefs governed the whole of my early life. I made my decisions based on them every day and in every situation. They still come up today, reminding me of the 'correct' decision to make or action to take. There is a little voice in my head that reminds me of these beliefs if I ever act against them.

Up until four years ago, I never believed that I was good enough at anything. I had no confidence in myself, and I hated drawing attention to myself. The prospect of public speaking was worse than death; I could never ever sit in the front row at an event, and I could never join in on a debate because I was too afraid of losing. Underneath it all lay one core belief: 'I am just not good enough.'

Having said that, I know I am a tough cookie, and I am determined and stubborn. I studied architecture in college because I thought of it as a man's job. I have been a buildings surveyor for the past 15 years, and my colleagues are 90 per cent male. This supports my belief that I can act like a man. I can go up ladders and get into lofts, and I can climb up scaffolding to look at roofs. This is my way of showing my grandma that I can do what a man can do.

I never say 'no' to my family or close friends because it is my mission to please everyone. I am scared of upsetting them and not winning their approval. I will always feel obliged to meet their requests even if it means I have to compromise my own schedule and wishes. This desire to please others cost me my home in 2010, and it has made me feel used and exhausted much of the time. I run around helping everyone but myself. I was hurt and disheartened many times but when I needed help, nobody came.

I did not marry a rich or handsome man; in fact, I deliberately avoided marrying anyone who fell into the category of being rich, handsome or popular because I believed that handsome or rich men were only meant to be with beautiful women, and I did not believe that I was either pretty or beautiful. I did not want to risk being hurt or ridiculed when my rich or handsome husband left me for someone else. The man I married does not challenge this belief. But don't get me wrong even though my husband may not be considered the most handsome man, he is the perfect man for me and the most wonderful father any child could have ever wanted.

How Can You Make Yourself Outstanding and Magnificent?

Now, it's possible that, like me, you have a personal belief system that may not be helping you. If that's the case, we need to review your belief system so we can identify any beliefs that no longer serve you. These are your limiting beliefs. Once you are aware of these limiting beliefs, you can begin to make a conscious decision to change or replace them with new beliefs that allow you to grow and expand.

Grab your journal then sit and relax. Take eight deep breathes and clear your mind of any worries or anxiety you may have. Draw a vertical line in the centre of a page to form two equal columns. In the left-hand column, write down your goals, dreams and desires. In the right hand columns, write down your response to the thoughts you have about your goals, desires and dreams. Here is an example:

My aspirations	My limiting beliefs
I want to earn £60,000 a year.	I do not have a degree, so I won't be able to earn that much money. No one will hire me at that level of income.
I want to be in the A-Team at netball.	I am not good at netball. My coach will never put me in the A Team.
I want to be all A-grade student	I am rubbish at science and history. I will never get A-grades for every subject.
I want to be debt-free.	I never have enough money to make ends meet. I will never be debt-free or at least it will be very hard for me to be completely debt free

I want to find my soul-mate	Nobody loves me, I am fat and ugly. I am not pretty or attractive enough
I want to have true friends	No one will be my true friend. I am not popular, pretty or clever enough. I do not know how to make people like me. Everything I do goes wrong.
I want to be a success-ful author	My writing is not good enough. No one will be interested in what I have to say.

Whatever you write in the right hand columns are your beliefs, or clues to your personal belief system. Now you have written down your beliefs, you can choose to change them from limiting beliefs to empowering beliefs. Doing this will change the course of your life. So next, cross out all your old beliefs and replace them with new empowering ones.

My Aspirations	Limiting belief	Empowering belief
I want to earn £60,000 a year	I do not have a degree, so I won't be able to earn that much money. No one will hire me at that level of income.	Although I don't have a degree, I can earn £60,000 a year if I wish. I don't need a degree to earn £60,000 a year
I want to be in the A Team for netball	I am not good at netball. My coach will never put me in the A Team.	I am an excellent netball player, and I will be in the A Team soon.
I want to be all A's student	I am rubbish at science and history, and I will never get A-grades for every subject.	I can achieve A-grades in any subject I choose. I am good at both history and science.
I want to be debt free	I never have enough money to make ends meet. I will never be debt-free or at least it will be very hard for me to be completely debt free.	I have all the money I need to cover all expenses with plenty residual income for what I want.
I want to find my soulmate	Nobody loves me, I am fat and ugly. I am not pretty or attractive enough.	Everyone loves me for who I am. I have a soulmate for life.

I want to have true friends	No one will be my true friend. I am not popular, pretty or clever enough. I do not know how to make people like me. Everything I do goes wrong.	Real friends accept me and love me for who I am. I am special and I have many true friends in my life.
I want to be a successful author	My writing is not good enough. No one will be interested in what I have to say	I have excellent materials for books. I am a successful author.

The new beliefs may sound like lies to you at first, but if you keep affirming them to yourself, they will eventually sink in and soon your subconscious mind will start to believe and accept every word as true. Once your subconscious mind accepts a statement to be true, the Universe will rearrange the scenery, the backdrop, players and events to make what you believe happen.

"If you change the way you look at things, the things you look at change."

WAYNE DYER

❊ *My Story*

As a female Building Surveyor, I believed that my career would be more challenging for me than for a man. I am used to having contractors and clients make sexist comments about my career. These comments made me doubt myself for many years, and I accepted lower pay and lower level roles because my beliefs and cultural conditioning led me to believe that male surveyors were naturally better than female surveyors.

In September 2012, I wrote in my journal, "I am the best surveyor this organisation ever employed. I am making £4,000 each month working from home." At the time, I was making £1,600 a month as a building surveyor. I worked as hard as the other (male) surveyors if not harder, and I did more and better quality work than them. After

I wrote that statement, I began to work on instilling new beliefs and thoughts into myself, and things began to change.

The situation at the organisation I worked for changed due to a corporate restructure, and I was forced to find another job after just a year in the job. I could have stayed if I wanted to, but I chose not to because I wouldn't have been able to do the school run. Hannah has always been more important than any job or thing in my life. The Universe also knew that if I was going to change, it would have to push the 'Hannah' button on me. I will tolerate anything, but as soon as Hannah is affected in any way or form, it's a game-changer.

My new job was a short term contract covering the role for someone who was off sick for a long-term. I took it. It was a 20-minute journey, but I was getting paid over £1,000 pounds a week. The short term contract lasted for 13 months and continued despite the person I was covering returned to work two months after I started. After the person who was sick returned to work, the office did not have a desk available for me so I was told that I could work from home! Suddenly, my diary entry had been manifested into real life.

By simply changing my beliefs, I also changed my thoughts and my life. As a result of this contract, my confidence went up because I received so many compliments and positive testimonials. This helped me to realise that I am good at what I do—I am a competent building surveyor and being a woman I can actually bring added qualities to the role.

Since then, I have earned more than £4,000 a month in every other contract I have ever had. I have never had a problem getting a job or a reference. This is a proof that your beliefs can be changed to serve you better. If you change your beliefs, you can make your life amazing and that will make you both magnificent and outstanding!

Your Conscious and Subconscious Minds

Before we go any further, I feel that it is important for me to introduce you to the concept of the conscious and subconscious minds. Of course, you only have one mind but within your mind, there are two clearly-defined parts.

The conscious mind is the part that gives you orders. It does all the reasoning and logical work. It analyses your environment, makes decision about what you want in life, and what you want to believe. For example, if you are given a mathematical question of 4590 ×23, it will be your conscious mind that will work out the answer. However, if you are asked what 1 + 1 makes, it will probably your subconscious mind that answers. This is because the sum 1 + 1 is something you know by heart. You have known it since you started kindergarten or even before, so it is 'filed' in your mind palace for future reference.

When the 'challenge' of calculating 1 + 1 comes up, your subconscious mind answers it immediately from your filing system without having to work it out logically. However, the first question is not so easy, and so you won't have learnt the answer beforehand. That means you have no reference for it in your mind-palace filing system, so the conscious mind will have to work out the answer for you, using logic and your knowledge of mathematics.

It is the subconscious mind that keeps you alive every second of the day by making sure your body functions as it should. It makes sure your heart pumps sufficient blood through your body so that you breathe and that your organs all function correctly. It ensures that images captured by your eyes are sent to your brain to be translated at lightning speed.

Your subconscious also helps you to learn and repeat mechanical tasks like driving a car. As soon as you have learnt to drive a car, your subconscious mind takes over whenever you get into a car. As a result, you don't have to think about when to put the clutch down, when to change gear and when to brake. You do it on autopilot. If you do the same journey every day, you will probably notice that you don't have to think about it after a while. Your subconscious mind drives for you; it knows you are going to take the next turn. So, it seems as if you do it on autopilot, but actually, it's your subconscious mind that is doing it for you.

It is your conscious mind that makes the initial decision to learn something, but once the skill or knowledge has been absorbed, it is your subconscious mind that allows you to remember it and use it. Once a new skill has been learnt or a decision made, it is filed away in the subconscious mind to maintain it or put it into action.

Your conscious mind is the captain of your ship and the subconscious mind is the crew that accepts and carries out the orders. The crew trusts the captain to give orders and instructions and to keep the ship on course. It will never argue with or doubt any instruction from the captain.

It doesn't matter whether the captain is sending good orders or bad, the crew will simply execute the orders without question. That means that if the captain sends a bad order, the ship could sink.

Your conscious mind is the master and your subconscious mind is the slave. Once your subconscious mind accepts an idea or suggestion, it gets to work, making sure the idea is manifested one way or another. We are constantly giving orders to our subconscious mind without always understanding what we are asking it for. We have the choice of either feeding our subconscious mind quality thoughts and ideas or bombarding it with poor decisions that cause us to live unfulfilled lives.

The choice is yours. You have the power to control your thought processes. You can give orders and suggestions that align with your goals, aspirations and dreams or that move you away from what you want. As soon as you issue an instruction, your subconscious mind will begin to execute it, so make sure all your orders are issued so you achieve what you want, not what you don't want.

CHAPTER THREE
Your Thoughts Create Your Life
心 想 事 成 · 萬 事 如 意

"Watch your thoughts, they become words; watch your words, they become actions; watch your actions, they become habits; watch your habits, they become character; watch your character, it becomes your destiny."

LAO TZE

YOUR THOUGHTS ARE magical because they create your life. This is a fact. Did you know that you have over 60,000 thoughts every day? Many of your thoughts run on auto-pilot, which means they very rarely change from one day to the other. This means that your life is more or less the same every day, too. Before you can change your life or have a different life, you need to change your thoughts.

Your current life is a manifestation of your thinking. This is because your thoughts emit vibrations. Every thought you think vibrates at a specific frequency and each frequency attracts or manifests specific events that have matching frequencies. Let's go back to the first day of my kindergarten in January 1980 to see how this works in reality.

On my first day, I very quickly established that my new classmates were laughing at me for being big. My form teacher made a comment about my appearance to Mama and I was standing in front of the whole class, feeling sick and awkward. I still remember that morning, and how I just wanted the ground to swallow me up. All I wanted was to vanish into thin air.

But my wish wasn't granted, and I was left there, standing in front of the class, looking at my new classmates. Suddenly, they looked tiny in comparison with me. I felt like an ogre and completely out of place. I just knew I didn't fit in and decided there and then that I would never fit in. They looked pretty, and I felt ugly.

After that experience, I dreaded going to school every day. I don't remember having any girlfriends that year. There was only one boy I recall playing with every day. He was my only friend at kindergarten. The girls laughed at me and teased me most of the time. Every day, I felt sad thoughts about going through yet another day at school and being a laughing stock. I anticipated bad things happening to me every day, and I started imagining over and over again what the girls would do to me.

I became obsessed with it, and lo and behold, my thoughts became my reality. Every day, my classmates made fun of me, so I felt sad and helpless and nothing changed. The Universe delivered to me what I thought about every day: pain, sadness, anger, hurt and distress. Those thoughts were manifested in the form of more teasing, rejection and bullying. It was a negative cycle: I got more of what I thought about. The Universe did not argue with my thoughts because I am the creator of my life, the captain of my ship. I get everything I ask for, whether it's good, bad or indifferent.

What are you thinking about at this moment? What have you been thinking about most recently? Have you been thinking about things that make you happy or unhappy? Have you been thinking thoughts of hope or loss? What do you want to experience in the days to come? You are the creator of your life, the master of your experiences, the captain of your ship–give the Universe and your subconscious the right orders or your ship will be wrecked.

This is the Law of Attraction, a law that is as real as the law of gravity. Whether or not you believe or acknowledge it, the law is in action without fail. As Mike Dooley famously pointed out, "Thoughts become things, choose the good ones."

'The Past' is not 'the Future', when you change your thoughts, you change your destiny.

Dear Hannah,

When I was a child, my world was very small. There was gong-gong and poh-poh, your three uncles (kao-fu), auntie (yi-yi), great grandma (tai-poh), my grandma (who you never met), the village, the school and the rest of my relatives. Gong-gong worked as a truck driver in the rainforest. His job was to transport tree trunks to the river so they could be floated downstream to the factory. I saw gong-gong twice a year at Chinese New Year and at Autumn Festival or what we Chinese call 'Mooncake Festival'. You've been to the village for the Mooncake Festival once, but I'm not sure if you still remember it. We lit candles and put them on tree branches around the house. You had a goldfish lantern that gong-gong bought for you.

Tai-poh (my grandmother) did not like me because I am a girl. My second brother, your Yin kao-fu was her favourite. Her 'Golden pomelo' (another Chinese expression). The others were just her grandchildren, neither here nor there as grandchildren numbers three, four or five do not really matter. The oldest child is supposed to be a boy so the bloodline can continue; otherwise the responsibilities of the family will fall onto the first son.

When I was a child, I was never given new toys or clothes because I was the oldest child. In Chinese culture, unless you are a boy, you are taught not to fight with your younger brothers or sister for toys, clothes, food, etc. In fact, I quickly learnt that it was me who must provide for my younger siblings. Until my brothers and sister were born, I was given new clothes and toys every year. I still remember the Scalextric set that gong-gong bought me; it was my favourite toy and quickly became my little treasure. I lost the privilege of being given new things when I had four brothers and sisters. Money was tight, and there was never enough to go round. As soon as Mun kao fu came along, I had to learn to accept that I would not be given any new clothes at Chinese New Year. My environment, culture and situation all demonstrated to me that there was not enough, and this was reinforced as the family grew. I grew up believing I was not worthy of prosperity because I was born a girl. I believed I was a disappointment to my family because not only was I a girl rather than a boy, but also I was the oldest child in my family!

My small world was constrained by this very old-fashioned thinking. Worse was that my world did not give me hope or the mind-set I needed to thrive or feel that there was ever enough. I believe that I was not worthy of anything, that no one cared about me and that I was lucky to get three meals a day and be allowed to go to school. I was told to be grateful and not to complain. New clothes were not for me.

Hush Puppies were not for me, even though I would have loved to have had a pair. I dared not ask for or expect anything good for myself just in case I was disappointed. I used to feel angry at my life. I used to wish I was a boy. I used to wish I was the only child. Everything seemed so unfair. I was told, 'this was your fate' and so there never seemed to be any way out.

I used to escape into my own world through my imagination. I used to re-enact the scenes I watched on television, pretending to be the hero saving the world or imagining that I was a genie who could make a pair of Hush Puppies magically appear in the blink of an eye. I fantasised about being rescued by a handsome prince or of travelling around the world on a flying carpet ... It was in these moments of imagination that I started to believe that there was another world out there. I was inspired by 'The adventures of Indiana Jones' and Disney's 'Cinderella' and 'Aladdin'. I was given hope by the success of Michelle Yeoh, Miss Malaysia 1983 who built a successful career in Hong Kong (She was the Bond Girl in 'Tomorrow Never Dies' in 1997). I was motivated by the iconic song NEW YORK, NEW YORK and I imagined what it would be like to live in a 'city that never sleeps'. Life was so dull that Popeye and Olive's life looked more interesting than mine!

When I was twelve, I decided that I needed to leave the village and go abroad. I didn't care whether I went to America or England. These were the only two countries I knew about outside of Malaysia, Singapore, Hong Kong

and Thailand. Geography was not my strongest point!
Yes, I know it sounds like I was living in a cave and to
be honest, at times, it felt like that too. I decided
that learning English was going to be my priority so
from then onwards I focused on getting good enough to
read and speak fluent English. I also decided that I
needed some luck so every night I knelt before a piggy
bank shaped like the Chinese Goddess of Mercy and
prayed that I would be able to go abroad when I grew up.
I asked The Goddess of Mercy to kindly change my fate.
After all, I was one of her many goddaughters so why
shouldn't she bless me?

Yes, I can see your reaction, baby, but let me explain.
In Chinese culture, when a new baby is born, the parents
dedicate the child to one of the Gods or Goddesses to
be blessed and so they can be kept safe and healthy,
and have a good life. So, like many children in our
culture, I was dedicated to the Goddess of Mercy as a
goddaughter. Of course, being from a Buddhist family,
we had a full-blown altar in our living room (as you
have seen when you've been back to the village). But as
my wish to go abroad was a secret one, I dared not
openly pray at the family altar in case someone heard
me. I just knew they would laugh at me so I couldn't risk
it. So, I ended up praying in secret to the piggy bank
instead.

In hindsight, I realise that when I was praying, my
thoughts were focused on the result I wanted. I saw
myself leaving my village, getting on a plane and flying

away. Some nights, I pretended I was flying to New York and other nights, I imagined myself flying to London (even though at that point in my life I had never been to an airport or on a plane). When I prayed to the piggy bank and imagined myself in other places, I felt happy and excited. In those moments, I truly believed that I was in New York or London. I felt free at last. My emotions changed from feelings of hopelessness to those of excitement. I went on an emotional journey from despair to joy.

What is amazing is that the Universe started to re-arrange things in response to these new thoughts and feelings. The people and events in my life started to change. I finished my education and went to college in Kuala Lumpur (all colleges are in the capital city). I found my first job and even though it was not the job I applied for, it worked out well for me. I joined a company that helped me to travel to the UK. I studied architecture and building so I applied for jobs with architects, but I was invited to an interview at Taylor Woodrow Projects, the main contractor for the Light Rail Transit System in Kuala Lumpur. They were looking for an AutoCAD Draughtsman. They offered me the job, and I took it.

The company was full of expats. There were engineers, project managers and construction managers from the UK. I have never seen so many 'kwai lo' in my life! But the job was great and it was the first time I felt appreciated for who I was. At the end of the contract, the project manager, Andrew Miles and the construction manager, David Whittingham helped me to transfer to UK. One of the contractors I got to know while working at Taylor Woodrow sponsored me so I could study when I got there. I believe that the Universe arranged this job for me and put me in a perfect situation to move to the UK. It rearranged the players in my life to ensure that my dreams would come true.

My life has not been the same since I decided to ask my piggy bank for what I wanted. Even so, it took 10 years for me to achieve my dreams, but when it happened the timing was perfect. I simply hadn't been ready before then and the right players had not been in place. From that I learnt that when the time is right, everything falls into place.

I started a new chapter in my life when I went to the UK in 1997. Since then, I have added a few more chapters to my Book of Adventures, and I am looking forward to the next ones just around the corner. This proved to me that the past does not equal the future. I realised I was able to decide to change my life and that if I changed my thoughts, I could change my destiny.

The same is true for you too, Hannah. My beautiful baby, this is your time to create your amazing life. Have faith, be courageous and hold on to your dreams. Never give up. I am here for you and will always be with you.

Lots of love, Mummy

CHAPTER FOUR
Emotions Are Your Guidance System

OUR EMOTIONS ARE closely linked to our perceptions and our perceptions shape our view of the world and of ourselves through our beliefs. They both are limiting and empowering. This is why your emotions are central to you being able to manifest the life you want. Our emotions influence the vibration of our thoughts and it is through these vibrations that we attract or repel what we most desire.

To see how this works for yourself, think of something that makes you happy, something you really want in life. Next, imagine you have it, right here, right now. How do you feel? Happy? Joyful? Grateful? When you are happy, joyful, grateful or feeling positive in any way, your vibrations around that particular thought climbs so high it will hit the roof? You can literally feel the energy of that thought! Next, think of something sad that has happened in your life. How do you feel? Sad, low, regretful? When you are feeling sad, the vibrations around the thought will be lower than when you had the happy thought, so will your energy level.

When these emotional vibrations are sent out to the Universe, it will attract events with the same vibrational and energy matter back into your life. These might be in the form of events, people or circumstances. This means that your highly-charged emotions with a high frequency of vibration will attract events, people or circumstances that match or share the same vibrational frequency. As I said earlier, every one of us has over 60,000 thoughts every day. This means when we think the same thoughts over and over again, we send out the same vibrational and energy levels to the Universe. This is why we keep attracting the same events, circumstances and people into our lives over and over again. It's the reason why our lives rarely change. Until we learn to guide our thoughts and emotions, we will continue to live the same life next year as we have for the past five years.

Do you have friends who worry about anything and everything? Do you have members of your family who are always sad? Have you had colleagues who are miserable, no matter what? Do you also know people who are always happy and seemingly not bothered by anything? Both of these groups of people behave the way they do due to their differing beliefs, thoughts and emotional platforms (the emotions that constantly affect someone).

What this shows is that someone who lives on a 'sad' emotional platform will tend to believe life is hard and full of sadness and will find it hard to see any joy in anything. When someone is sad, their whole posture, breathing and thinking will be affected making it hard for them to do anything productive or positive. Do you know a sad person? How does he usually look? Can you feel his sadness when you are in his company? Does he stand up straight? How does he walk? How does he speak? Is it quickly or slowly? What is his tone of voice like? Is it quiet or loud?

Next, think of someone who lives on a 'happy' emotional platform. What is her attitude to life? Do you think she will get upset easily? Of course not! Happiness is an inside job and often takes a major disaster or tragedy to shift this person from happiness to sadness. When you think of someone you know who is always happy, can you recall how they look? Is she smiling? Does she speak quickly or slowly? Does she speak loudly or quietly? What is her posture? Does she sit up straight? How does she walk?

As you can see from this, emotions affect our entire being and are the key ingredients in enabling us to create and manifest our dream life. As Andy Dooley brilliantly said: "Feeling First, Manifestation Second."

Emotions: LOVE 愛

To me, 'love' is a beautiful word because without love, life is meaningless. There are three categories of love; unconditional love, conditional love and self-love or loving yourself. Let's look at each of them in turn now.

Unconditional Love

'Unconditional love' or 'infinite love' refers to the love we receive from God or the Universe. Whether you believe in God or not, I am sure you will accept that God's love is unconditional. God and the Universe love us just as we are without any reservations or conditions. Unconditional love is a gift. It is not contingent upon time, space or matter. It is part of our inheritance as a result of being created in the image of God.

Who is God? Personally, I do not believe that God is a 'big guy' sitting up there in the sky watching us and passing judgement on what we do every day. I do not believe God is who we are led to believe he (or she) is. Over the years, religions have put God into a box and created hundreds or even thousands of rules in his (or her) name. These rules are based on the agendas of many influential believers and leaders, such as monks, pastors, priests, nuns and imams.

Don't get me wrong; I've got nothing against religion, and I know the leaders of many religions are doing their best to introduce their ideas about God to believers and non-believers. Every religion believes their God is the true God but I believe that God needs to be given a free hand to do his job. Let God be God. After all, he is the Creator of this magical Universe and everyone, everything within it.

Hannah, do you remember asking me, "Where does God live?" And do you remember what I told you? I said, "God lives in here", and put my hand on your heart because God lives in you and in me. You are of God; you are made in the image of God. It is because you belong to God. You cannot be anything else but the eyes and ears of God. You are born with the characteristics of God. It is fair to say that you are a spiritual being having a human experience.

I was born and raised in a Chinese family or maybe I should say, "I chose to be born into a Chinese family who practise Buddhism". Growing up in Malaysia, I was exposed to other religions, such as Islam, Christianity, Taoism and Hinduism. From my experience, every religion represents God as the source of unconditional love, kindness, spirituality, pureness, joy, peace, forgiveness, fairness, omnipotence, grace, and everything that is pure and good. Where there is chaos and war allegedly in the name of Islam or Christianity or Taoism, it is simply an extreme example of what I mentioned earlier in this chapter; members of various religions interpreting the teaching of their 'God' to suit their own agendas. They then manipulate people to believe in the so-called rules they create so they can control their victims using fear, confusion, force or pure lies.

In this cyber age, I do not know what you will come across in the future, Hannah, but I want to be very clear that whatever you hear or do or see, you must believe and have faith that God represents unconditional LOVE, God is LIFE. and God will never ever DESTROY or HARM life in any shape or form. Unconditional means there are no expectations or conditions, and you never have to do anything to earn God's love. Hence, God is a God of freewill. He does not impose thoughts or actions on your life. He knows that you have chosen your life on earth, and you are here to learn, to explore and to enjoy the most amazing adventure possible in time and space.

However, God will always be there when you need him. All you have to do is ask. God is always there for you, me and everyone who seeks him. His help will always be just a stone's throw away. Most of the time, he is right outside your front door waiting for you to let him in because he loves you just as you are! It is down to you to open your doors, windows and your heart so you can accept his help. If you get caught up in your own dramas and the pressures of life, you might not see that his help is there. You might shut out the world because you are preparing to lock down your mind palace and hide away from the world. You may have surrendered, too exhausted to go on and too depleted to see the path in front of you. If you are ever in such a situation, have faith and know that GOD loves you unconditionally. Have the courage to ask for help. There is no catch! Unconditional love is absolute; there is no escape, even if you want to escape.

Conditional Love

Conditional love is slightly different from unconditional love. This is the love that is experienced between spouses, family members, friends, colleagues and acquaintances. Conditional love is an emotion based on events and circumstances that are bound in time and space. It changes depending on the perceptions and beliefs you hold at any particular time in your life. There are conditions that must be met before we share our love or earn the love we yearn for. You may think that the love between a mother and child is unconditional. But is it? In general, mothers love their children no matter what happens and will forgive their children almost anything. However, I believe there is a point where the love will be affected or even broken and that's when the expectations or conditions desired by the mother or child are not met.

Self-Love or Loving Yourself

I find this the most difficult category of love to achieve. Self-love or loving yourself is something most of us are not trained to do. I have noticed a lot of resistance in people when this topic comes up at my seminars.

First, what does it mean to love yourself? How do you love yourself? In the UK, people use the phrase 'he loves himself' or 'she loves herself' to describe someone who is narcissistic, boastful and arrogant. So when I ask people at my seminars to love themselves, they are not keen. The first thoughts they have are of all the negative connotations they are familiar with in relation to self-love. I have made the same request from my audience in a number of places, including a church, but I always get the same reaction from the audience.

The late Louise Hay says, "Loving ourselves is having great respect for ourselves and gratitude for the miracle of our bodies and our minds". But self-love is not about arrogance or boastfulness. It is about accepting yourself just as you are. Do you remember that at the start of this book we firmly established that you are special? The very first step to loving yourself is to believe that you are special just the way you are!

Loving yourself means:
- Feeling joy about your life.
- Feeling grateful that you are alive.
- Treating yourself with respect.
- Taking good care of your body, mind and soul.
- Accepting that you learn from mistakes rather than getting bogged down with negative emotions.
- Enjoying your life, environment, family, friends and pets.
- Accepting help, compliments and gifts with grace and gratitude.

In contrast, let's look at what you do when you do not love yourself:
- Constantly criticise yourself.
- Marry someone for the wrong reasons.
- Blame yourself for everything that does not go well or for mistakes you make.
- Abuse your body, mind and soul with food, alcohol, drugs and casual sex.
- Belittle yourself because you are convinced you are not good enough.
- Persistently attract illness, failure and lack as a result of negative thinking.

- Fail to stand up for what you believe.
- Complain about your life endlessly.
- Reject help, compliments and gifts because you feel unworthy.

I think many of us, including me, often feel unable to love ourselves because we are afraid of upsetting the status quo, even though it causes us discomfort. We take the easy way out by giving in to peer pressure or the desire to please others. At my seminars, I ask my audience whether they criticise themselves? They answer:

- "Of course I criticise myself, everyone does it."
- "It is healthy to criticise myself."
- "It is a noble and humble thing to do."
- "I am not perfect so I criticise myself so that I can improve."

Next, I ask them how often they criticise themselves? They answer:

- "Every day."
- "Every minute."
- "Often."
- "When things go wrong or do not go according to plan."

So I ask them, why they criticise themselves? They say:

- "Because I am stupid."
- "Because I am too fat."
- "Because I am too short."
- "Because I am too tall."
- "Because I am too skinny."
- "Because I am too ugly."
- "Because I am too late."
- "Because I am too old."
- "Because I am too young."
- "Because no one respects me."
- "Because I am a failure."
- "Because I am not good enough."
- "Because I am not wealthy enough."

- "Because my wife tells me I'm no good."
- "Because my parents said I am a disappointment to them."
- "Because I do not have a degree."
- "Because I am rubbish at science."
- "Because my teacher said I am useless."
- "Because I am not earning enough."

Most of us learn to live by rules that dictate who we should be or how we should live our lives. It's part of the conditioning we receive as we grow up: you should do this, you should be that. Here are some examples:

- You should be at college or university.
- You should be married by now.
- You should be a successful businessman or women.
- You should be making a million pounds a year by the age of 40.
- You should be a doctor, a pilot, a teacher or a lawyer.
- You should have bought a house of your own by now instead of renting.

"You should, you should, and you should."

These expectations and rules create what I call the blueprint of your life. It seems as if this blueprint is set in stone, but it can be changed, and I will show you how to do that here.

First of all, you must begin to believe you are special just as you are. There is nothing you 'should' do or 'should' be at any time in your life. Don't 'should' yourself all the time. Let's cut the word 'should' out of our vocabulary from this moment onwards. Let's learn to live our lives on our own terms. Look into a mirror and look closely at the person staring back at you. Tell the person, "I am sorry that I have neglected you all these years. I'm sorry that I have forgotten to love you and to care for you. Please forgive me. Thank you for never giving up on me, thank you for loving me. I love you." Appreciate those eyes, love those lips, and marvel at the beautiful features of your face: your nose, your chin, your cheeks, your forehead, your hair, eyebrow, and freckles—the lot! Be grateful that you are who you are and that you are alive.

Papa always says, "Your appearance comes from your heart."

How you seem or how you look, is a reflection of what is inside of you, what is in your hearts and what you think about. It has nothing to do with how much make-up you put on every day, whether you have the latest hairstyle or whether you wear designer clothing. Have you ever met or seen people who are dressed to the nines yet they appear to be unattractive, sad or even unkind? It is because the essence of who you are comes through in your face and your behaviour. It took me many years to grasp this, and it's why Papa says, "To be beautiful on the outside, you must be beautiful on the inside first."

When we love and respect ourselves, those so-called problems will no longer be problems. The fat will melt away without you having to diet, your skin blemishes will clear away, you will glow with health and your finances will improve. Everything will get better, from your exam grades to your social life, and your love life will be as good as you want it to be. Why? Because when you love and respect yourself you will have inner peace, true happiness, confidence and love. This will raise your emotional and thought vibrations to extraordinary heights. Remember, your emotional platform is built on joy, excitement and happiness. People will sense your vibrations when they are high. They will feel your joy and excitement. You will be glowing, and you will attract the events and people that match those vibrations and make it possible for you to create a wonderful life.

❋ *My Story*

At the time of writing this book, I am working as a full-time freelance Project Manager. I take on temporary contracts ranging from two to 18 months. I have just finished a five-month contract where I was paid £80 an hour. There was a three-week gap after that contract ended and so I went for an interview as an Assistant Project Manager. After the interview, the agency representing me called to tell me the client wanted to offer me the job. They asked me to tell them my hourly rate. I told them it was £25 but as I knew the job was advertised at £20-£24 per hour, I said I wanted £24 per hour. The agency then tried to convince me to take the contract at £22 per hour, saying that the client would give approval immediately at this rate so allowing me to start the following Monday. I reluctantly agreed to this but gave one condition: the client must agree to pay me for all the hours I worked. If I worked 40 hours in a week, they must pay me for 40 hours. The agency went back to the client, and it was agreed.

So, on the first week of the contract, I ended up working 38.5 hours and I submitted my timesheet for this number of hours. But to my surprise, the client told me to adjust the figures to 37 hours instead as these were the hours I was contracted to work. They said they would not pay me for working the extra time and that any extra hours I worked would be at my own expense!

I felt betrayed and angry. I felt they had used me and taken advantage of me. When I called the agency and told them what had happened, the agency told me I must not work more than 37 hours a week. I was shocked. Only a few days ago the agency said it had been agreed with the client that they would pay me whatever hours I worked, and now they were telling me that I must stick to 37 hours a week. I was furious! I fumed all the way home and kept replaying the conversations I'd had with the agent in my mind over and over again. I relived the scene repeatedly, cursing the agency for such deceit. I scolded myself for being stupid enough to believe a 'salesman' and I berated the client for going back on their word. I told myself I was a victim and that I had been deceived … and so on and so forth. The little devilish voice of negativity and rage went on and on and on. I was concentrating on this event so much that I was drove home on autopilot. I'm surprised I got home safely!

The agency offered to speak to client about the issue, but I was worried about what would happen if they did. I hate confrontation. I reasoned that if I let things go this way I would end up working with the client for the next three months feeling cheated and angry because I didn't want to create bad feeling over an hour's pay. The indecision went on and on: *should I let the agency speak to the client, or not? It was a condition they agreed to before I accepted the contract,* I thought, *so they should honour it*. It is a matter of principle. *Should I speak to client myself as I do not trust agency anymore?* Now, the client not only gets a Project Manager for the price of an Assistant Project Manager, they're not even going to pay for all the hours I work! So it went on. I was in such a muddle that I didn't know what to think or do.

When I calmed down, I realised it was nobody's fault but my own that this had happened. If only I had loved myself more, I would not have been in this situation. I did not love myself enough to ask for the appropriate fee for my services. I did not love myself enough to stand up for what I believed to be true. I did not love myself enough to accept that I deserved better.

You see, I have 15 years of experience in my field, I have a proven track record of successful project management and control of building work and great technical knowledge, but I did not love myself enough to see that I deserved a better role. Instead of applying for the Project Manager position, I went for an Assistant Project Manager position. I put myself down just by doing that. It was a demoralising feeling.

If I loved myself truly and completely, I would have stuck to my fee of £25 an hour. I would not have let the agency talk me into believing that I did not deserve £25 an hour or into believing that I would lose the contract if I did not agree to the request for a lower fee. If I had stuck to my guns about the £25 an hour fee, I would not have set the condition on being paid for the extra hours, which means the entire incident about the extra hour would not have happened in the first place. I had learnt my lesson the hard way, but the experience stayed with me, and I know I will never put myself down in the same way again.

Please do not put yourself down as I did. It is soul-destroying. There are many people out there who are more than ready to squash you without a second thought. You will find them everywhere: at school, college, university or when you are stepping out and starting your first job—or even your fifteenth. Do not do it to yourself. In fact, be on your guard against it. Stay away from these people. Do not give them the opportunity to put you down or manipulate you into thinking you are anything other than very special. You deserve the best so love yourself fully, truly and completely.

Emotions: HATRED 恨

"Hatred does not cease by hatred, but only by love; this is the eternal rule."

BUDDHA

Hate is a very strong word because it represents a strong emotion—an emotion that has the power to destroy everything around it. But hate cannot exist without love. If there is no love, there can be no hate. Hate is the opposite of love and arises between people when the conditions needed for love are not met or when a person is rejected. The love between parents and children, brothers and sisters, relatives, friends and colleagues is contingent upon their behaviour and actions so it's not unconditional love. Depending on the strength of the emotions involved and the conditions surrounding the relationship, feelings can easily change from love to disappointment and then to hurt, anger, embarrassment, frustration, blame, jealousy and finally hatred.

When you feel hatred towards someone, you are letting that person live in your head rent free. Hate is an emotion that feels like a parasite that slowly destroys your mind, body and soul. Hatred causes illness, and it stops you from enjoying your life. Never allow anyone to bring hatred into your life. You have a choice. You are in control. When someone you love lets you down or is unable to meet your expectations, forgive them. They did their best at that particular time and in that particular situation. They did their best based on their personal belief system and perceptions.

Emotions: FEAR 恐懼

"Fears are nothing more than a state of mind."

NAPOLEON HILL

To me, fear is a strange emotion. Our common sense tells us fear is scary and something to be avoided. It is the big bad wolf of the emotional world because it cripples you, stops you in your tracks and makes you feel sick. In reality, though, fear is an emotion that can help to catapult us to success so that we reach our goals. That's if we use it well. Everyone experiences fear around something. What makes you feel afraid? How does your fear stop you from doing something or prevent you from trying something new? Let me share some of the fears I used to have:

- Fear of rejection.

- Fear of losing someone or something.
- Fear of attracting attention.
- Fear of public speaking.
- Fear of embarrassment.
- Fear of getting hurt.
- Fear of making the wrong decision.

With so many fears, it's no wonder I didn't get very far in life! There are other types of fears too, for example:

- Fear of flying.
- Fear of confined spaces.
- Fear of the dark.
- Fear of heights.
- Fear of spiders.
- Fear of snakes
- Fear of creepy crawlies

The list is endless, because it's possible to be afraid of almost anything. This is because fears are generated by our personal belief systems and these influence our perceptions of the world. This is another good example of when our beliefs are hindering us rather than serving us in achieving our goals and desires.

I urge you not to give in to your fears. Face them and use them to improve your life. You can conquer your fears by looking at them square in the face and challenging yourself to do what you fear. If this sounds too hard, you might want to take some smaller steps first.

1) The first thing you can do to remove your fear is to reason it away. Feed it with facts and statistics until your subconscious mind accepts that this particular fear is not a threat to your life. Convince your subconscious mind that you do not need protection from this particular thing or situation.

2) The second option is to use affirmations. To make them work, you must make sure you say your affirmations with feeling and that you believe what you are affirming. Simply reciting an affirmation over and over without thought, feeling or faith will not

remove your fear. In fact, it will make it worse so make sure you mean every single word.

3) The third option is my favourite, and it gets my adrenalin pumping sky high every time. It is a wonderful experience. In my opinion, it is the most effective way of conquering your fear. It is (in Susan Jeffers' words) to 'feel the fear and do it anyway!' There is another step I like to add to this, and that is to feel the fear, acknowledge it and then do what you were going to do anyway. For example, if you have a fear of public speaking, set out to find an opportunity to do a small presentation in a safe environment. When you've done it, you'll be really proud of your achievement, and you might wonder what all the fuss was about!

Emotions: GRATITUDE 感謝

Life is wonderful! It is a gift! But you might not always agree when life isn't going well for you, for example when you've lost someone or something precious to you or when things are just not working out for you. It took me many years to learn that gratitude is your best ally for manifesting your bliss or creating the life of your dreams. This is because what you focus on expands. That is the more you focus on something with grati-tude, the more good things will be attracted to you.

Every year, on the eve of Chinese New Year, Mama warned us not to frown, argue or complain about anything. We were told not to lose our temper or cry—we were especially warned against crying! For the next three days, all we were allowed to do was smile and laugh all the time. No other emotions were allowed, whether we liked it or not. This is because Mama's (like most Chinese people) believe that if we smile and are happy for the first three days of Chinese New Year, the God of Fortune will bless our household for the entire year! Anyone who buys a lottery ticket will win, and anyone who has a job or career can expect a promo-tion and pay rise. The household will be blessed and prosperous in every way for the entire year!

When I was in my teens, I discovered that it is not just being happy during Chinese New Year that brings good fortune. Mama didn't explain this to us when we were children, but the key to good fortune is to be grateful for what you have all the time. Chinese people believe that we always have everything we need at any given moment in life so we can always be grateful for our family being complete and whole as that is all that matters during Chinese New Year.

The Chinese New Year's eve dinner is the most important dinner of the year. It is called the Reunion Dinner and every single family member is expected to be home for it. That is the start of the Chinese New Year celebrations, when the family is home, complete and whole. At this time in particular, we are taught to be grateful for 'angpow', food, friends and the time we spend together. Mama believes when we are grateful for all this, more will come. Mama is always winning the lottery! I am not kidding—I have no idea how she does it. Last year, Mama and Papa both won over 10,000 Malaysian ringgit over Chinese New Year. Whenever Mama is a bit low on funds, nine out of ten times, she will win money through the lottery, though, sometimes those sums are more substantial than others!

Another example of the power of gratitude is the feeling it gives you when you are thanked by others. Can you recall the time when you've done something for someone you love and they give you heart-felt 'thanks'? How do you feel when that happens? Do you feel you want to do more for them? Do you feel good about yourself because you are appreciated by them? Do you feel happy because you have done something that has made a difference to someone else? I'm sure, if they needed you again in the future, you would not hold back from helping them again—in fact, you may even step it up a notch and do even more. That's the power of gratitude!

This is how gratitude works with the Universe, as well. The more gratitude you show, the more the Universe will deliver what you want. The only difference between the Universe and other people is that the Universe's love is unconditional, so it is GUARANTEED. The more grateful you are for what you have the more likely it is that better things will come. It may take time, but when it arrives, it is better than we ever hoped or imagined.

What could you be grateful for in this moment? List at least 10 things you are grateful for in your life right now? To help get you started, take a look at some of the things I am grateful for in my life:

- I am truly grateful for my beautiful daughter, Hannah.
- I am truly grateful for my wonderful husband, David.
- I am truly grateful for my life.
- I am grateful for the air I breathe.

- I am grateful for all the money I receive and all the money that is yet to come to me.
- I am grateful for my ever-supportive and ever-loving Mama and Papa, who never stop loving me.
- I am grateful for my amazing sister, Phui Kuan, the best sister anyone could ask for.
- I am grateful for all my brothers, and for sharing their lives with me.
- I am truly grateful for the continuous supply of job contracts I receive.
- I am grateful for all my true friends.
- I am grateful for the opportunity to write this book.
- I am grateful for the Universe, which always supplies all my needs.
- I am grateful for our cute tortoise, Truffle. It brings us joy and laughter watching it.
- I am grateful for all the holidays we have enjoyed.
- I am truly grateful for my good health.
- I am grateful for the beautiful colour of the sea, the waves and the breeze.
- I am grateful for the journal that I am using.
- I am grateful for the lifestyle that I enjoy.

Take a piece of paper or if you have one, your journal and write down what you are grateful for in your life at this moment in time. I challenge you to come up with 100 things you are grateful for. Start each statement with, 'I am grateful for…' or 'I am truly grateful that…' Notice how you feel when you write these statements. Remember, what you focus on expands. The more you can find to be grateful for right now, the more great events will be attracted to you—and then your gratitude will increase even more. It's a wonderful upward spiral of gratitude and blessings.

Emotions: ANGER 怒

"There is nothing wrong with anger, providing you use it constructively."

WAYNE DYER

Let me tell you a secret, 'no one can make you angry'. I know you're looking at me now as if I'm mad but you hear me right, 'no one can make you angry'. You have to allow others to make you angry. You have to give them consent or permission to make you angry. You have to let them into your head.

This is true for all your emotions, not just anger. No one can make you feel anything; you do that yourself.

Why or when do you get angry? You probably get angry when you feel you have lost control of a situation, when you feel you have been misunderstood, when you feel you have been victimised or when you believe your position is at risk or is being invaded one way or another. I get angry when:

- Hannah disobeys me, or I think she has been disrespectful to me.
- Difficult clients are unreasonable or verbally abusive, and I am unable to retaliate because of company policy.
- My position is compromised due to the betrayal of others.
- I experience continuous frustrations, and things do not go according to the plan.
- I am angry at God for not answering my prayers, despite my persistent requests!
- Family members demand my help without any thought as to my well-being.
- I perceive that my friends are taking advantage of me.
- No one believes me.
- I found out I was being lied to.
- I made mistakes and hurt someone.
- I did not do what I meant to do in a situation and as a result caused hurt or pain to someone I love.

- I did not seize an opportunity when it was presented to me.
- I felt humiliated.

As you can see, there are a whole range of situations when I have allowed myself to react badly or get angry with myself or others. But anger can be managed, and I try to do this because I believe it is best to avoid getting angry.

When we look at these examples, you can see that each situation has been created by my perception that something or someone has not performed as well as I expected. Someone or something has not been good enough or they have done something that I perceived as wrong, unfair or unreasonable. It's the same for all of us, as all these events are in our heads, not in real life. It is our belief system that is causing us to judge a situation or a person's behaviour, and it is this that triggers our anger, leading us to react. Let me explain.

✳ *My Story*

A few years ago, I agreed to use my skills to help a friend take on a home renovation project. She wanted an extension to her house and so I helped with the drawings, schedule of works, tendering processes and getting the project set up on site. During the process, she kept changing her mind about what she wanted. She did this many times, making the scheduling and planning very difficult. Ultimately, this affected the cost of the project.

We got to the stage where the contractor who had won the tender phoned me to say that my friend had changed her mind yet again. I expressed my frustration to him about the entire project and told him it had been the same the whole way through. She had changed her mind over and over again and that this would be the fifth alteration she had made to the plans so far. I told the contractor that I was feeling very annoyed.

Two days later, I got a phone call from my friend. She started interrogating me about the conversation I had with the contractor. She asked why I had told him that she was difficult and asked why I was angry with her. I was furious to discover that the contractor had betrayed my trust and repeated our conversation. I reacted badly to the situation and, as a result, my conversation with my friend did not end well. She decided that I was no longer her friend because she thought I had 'slagged her off' in front of the contractor. At first, it was quite a relief that I was no longer helping her with the project as it had not been an easy job. But on the down side, the result is that I have not spoken to this friend since that phone call. I also found out that the work she wanted to do did not go ahead in the end so she still doesn't have the extension she wanted.

My angry reaction resulted in me losing a friend. She was not a close friend or someone I see every week but, still, she was my friend. If I could have seen that my friend was doing the best she could at that moment in time, I would not have reacted the way I did. I may not have been angry that she kept changing her mind all the time. I thought she was being difficult, that is why I reacted the way I did and allowed myself to get angry. The truth of the situation was that she had never taken on a project like that before and so it was understandable that she was anxious and wanted to get it right. She was doing the best she could and the best she knew at that moment in time. If I had seen this at the time, my friend would have had completed extension by now and I, probably, would have been a frequent visitor to her home and enjoyed many chats and cups of tea!

It is important that you remember that everyone is doing their best at any given moment in time and in any situation. Their actions or behaviour may not match what you believe they should be, but it is their belief system, that is guiding them. You need to acknowledge that everyone behaves, reacts, sees or does things in their own unique way.

When an unreasonable customer or client is dishing out verbal abuse to you due to their frustration, just remember that he or she is doing the best he or she can in a stressful situation. Perhaps his or her belief system is saying, "If I want something done, I need to shout and yell." You may not agree with that belief, but it is what your customer believes to be right. They do not know any other way. If you give this customer permission to get inside your head and make you angry, it is you that gets hurt emotionally and it is your vibrations that are affected. When you focus on anger, you will get more anger coming into your life. If you replay the scene while driving home (as I did), you will fume all the way so you arrive feeling low and annoyed. You have a lot to lose by being angry—it's just not worth it.

Of course, at the same time, it is important not to suppress your anger. Instead, feel your anger but try to understand why or what has triggered your feelings. Accept that everyone is doing their best at any given time and in every situation, even though you may not agree with their behaviour. Release the anger but do not re-enact it. Go home and hit a pillow, scream out loud at the sea, go for a long run, or do Zumba or Body Combat at your gym. Release every single ounce of the anger; never suppress it or let it brew inside you because anger can cause illness. Not only this, remember that it also attracts more undesirable events and people into your life. If you can learn to control your anger, you will have mastered one of the most important traits needed to conquer the world!

"You will not be punished for your anger, you will be punished by your anger."

BUDDHA

Emotions: GUILT 罪

What is guilt, and why do we feel guilty? Every one of us has our personal belief system and within this belief system, we have a section called 'character blueprint'. In this blueprint, we have a list of 'shoulds' and 'musts' that we set out for ourselves based on what we believe to be appropriate or right. In my character blueprint, which I believe is the same as many others, is the rule that I must be honest, helpful, kind, trustworthy, responsible and so on. I also have a 'milestone blueprint' for my life: I should be married by the age of 24; I should own a property by the age of 30; I should have a car when I am 18; I should have £300,000 in my saving account by the time I am 40; I should have this; I should do that—I 'should' all over myself!

Do you think I stand any chance of abiding by all these rules? That's a big, fat, NO! I am good most of the time, but I have done some 'not so good' things, too. I am not proud of these 'not so good' things as they violated the blueprint I hold of my character and my life. When I don't follow the blueprint, or I violate my own rules, it causes conflict in my mind (Where the blueprint is kept) and my heart (The core of my being). This evokes the 'guilt' within me. I feel guilty because I believe I have done something 'wrong', something that goes against my blueprint. It's the same for you as well. We all have a blueprint for ourselves, and rules that we make for our behaviour.

The blueprint is a benchmark we use to judge ourselves. We tell ourselves that if we abide by all our rules, we will be good, happy and safe. In truth, nothing could be further from the truth. For most of us, this tool actually achieves the complete opposite of what we believe it does. This is because when it is not used correctly (And not many of us know how to use it for our own benefit), we end up feeling disappointed, guilty, frustrated, anxious, fearful and depressed, amongst other things. However, when we understand or are able to unlock the code of our blueprints, it can become an extremely useful tool for manifesting more of our dreams and goals. Now, let's look at guilt in more details so we understand it and deal with it better.

❊ *My Story*

I am not short of stories about my own guilt because I have done so many things that I'm not proud of. Some things I will never tell anyone about because they are events that have caused me and others embarrassment, humiliation and hurt, all leading to guilt and heart- wrenching disappointment.

The first time I ever felt guilty was when I was very young. I lived in Kuantan and I was in year three at primary school, so I was around nine years old. My best friend was Ngoh. I do not remember the reasons or details, but one day we just decided to give a pair of twins a hard time at school. They were very cute, and they were two years younger than us. I cannot remember their names but we were bully-ing them! Yes, I was a horrible bully, and I am not proud of myself for this. Ngoh and I have never spoken about this since, but we got caught and the headmaster called us to his office and gave us a good talking to. We were made to stand outside the headmaster's office for half a day. It was the longest half day of our lives. I felt so guilty about the entire event. Thirty-three years on and recalling the event for this book, I still feel ashamed and guilty about what I did. I wish I could turn back time and do things differently. I can assure you that

I never bullied anyone ever again. In fact, I have made it my personal mission to always stand up for those who are being bullied.

Another time, I experienced guilt was when I was 12 or 13. My family had moved back to our village, and my school was an hour away from the village by road. That meant I had to get up at five-thirty in the morning so I could leave at six to catch the school bus. As there is only one bus from the village to the school, the driver usually tried to do the trip as short as possible. He used to drop the older children off in the town near the school. I liked getting off the bus in town because there were places to have snacks, and there was a supermarket called Parkson Grand.

I went to Parkson Grand every day after school and, at some point, I started to shoplift. Now, I can't remember what made me decide that I want to try out shoplifting, but I did. All I remember was that around that time in my life, I started to steal from the shop. At first, it was once a week but later it increased to twice a week. I took several things at a time, at least five or six items. The things I stole ranged from baby shoes for my sister to tins of food. I told Mama that I had won these silly prizes in a quiz at school, and she believed me.

This went on for a couple of months, but I felt so guilty when I lied and gave those 'prizes' to Mama. Mama was very pleased with me and proud of me, thinking that she had such a clever daughter winning all those prizes. I thought this was my chance to gain Mama's love and attention again. At that point, my youngest sister had just joined our family, and she was getting all the attention from everyone. I was just left to be. So, when mama was pleased, I thought it was my chance to claim back my position within the family.

As well as feeling apprehensive, guilty and scared, my adrenaline was also pumping whenever I prepared to walk into Parkson Grand. Each time, I told myself that I would do it just one more time and then I would tell Mama there would be no more quizzes at school. Despite the guilt, earning Mama's love and approval seemed to be more important to me. It was easier to bury the guilty feelings and just hope that I never got caught.

But, lo and behold, I did get caught! One day, when I had pilfered my goods and was walking out of the front door, a man came and grabbed me by the arm. He asked me to go with him as he dragged me along to the Manager's office. I wasn't in a position to refuse. When I arrived at the Manager's office, a stern face was staring at me.

He wasn't pleased, but there was sympathy in his eyes. He asked me why I did it. I told him, I don't know. I then pulled out around 56 Ringgit from my pocket and offered it to the manager. I said to him, "Look, I have money to pay for it. Please don't tell my Mum." I can't remember all the details of that meeting, I just know that he took the money I owed, and he let me go home. He did not phone the police or Mama. I felt guilty but very relieved at the same time.

Why did I do it? I just can't remember. I had money so I didn't need to steal, and I have never stolen or taken anything without permission since that day. In fact, a few years later, I took a part-time job to subsidise my college fund and caught a colleague fiddling the daily cash receipts from the business so she could cream off the extra money. She had been stealing from the business for years. I saw loopholes in the business procedures, such as the way the sales were registered each day. This colleague (I'll call her Sharon but that's not her real name) had been at the company for eight years when I joined, and she had been fiddling the sales receipts and cash register the whole time. I took it upon myself to investigate by doing a daily account every day after everyone had gone home. I did this for a whole month. I found out there was discrepancy between Sharon's daily account and mine. By the end of the month, I found over 900 ringgits were missing. I presented my findings to the boss, and they started their own investigation. Eventually, Sharon was asked to leave.

Let me share a more recent event with you. In 2005, my younger brother (the eldest boy in my family and referred to as the 'Golden Pomelo' by my grandma) arrived in the UK. I found him a job at our local Malaysian restaurant as a kitchen porter. While he was working there, he befriended a woman called Pang who was also a friend of the restaurant owner. My brother, Yin, started to complain about the job after just two weeks of doing it. Over the next year, he complained that the head chef was mean, that he had to do all the menial tasks, that he never received any thanks or praise for his work, that he never got a pay rise, and so on.

A year later, Yin came to see me to ask if I would act as Director of a company. He was setting up this company for a restaurant he was opening in Portsmouth. Pang was investing the money to buy a lease for the restaurant, and all they needed was a name on the paperwork to set up a limited company. My husband was against it because of the financial risk I was taking, but I just accused my husband of being unkind to my family. I believed I was obliged to help my brothers, sister and parents. I was programmed to stand by my family because I was the eldest child in the family. I trusted my brother and stood up for him. I insisted that I would help Yin, and I ignored my husband's advice and dismissed his concerns.

Initially, the restaurant seemed to be doing well. I set up direct debits through the bank to cover the main bills, and Yin and Pang dealt with the day-to-day running of the business. But in 2007, alarm bells started to ring when one Saturday morning bailiffs appeared at our door chasing unpaid business rates. It turned out that Yin and Pang had left the UK with £32,000 from the business and left huge debts in my name.

For three years after the bailiffs appeared at our door, me, my husband and my daughter lived in fear. We dared not answer the door unless we were expecting someone. We unplugged our home phone, and mail was left unopened. I was terrified, and the situation was hopeless. I eventually decided to go bankrupt in 2010. We lost our home, my car, and I lost my dignity. When I told my employer that I was bankrupt, I was suspended from my job. My employer then started a witch hunt in an effort to find fault with my work so he could dismiss me.

Deciding to back my brother is the biggest regret of my life. I felt enormously guilty for letting down my husband and daughter and for putting them through such a horrendous experience—and all because I chose to stick with my belief that blood is thicker than water and that my brother would never hurt or harm me. I still feel guilty now, and I desperately want to make amends. It is my mission to provide my husband and daughter with a dream home and the best I can afford. I have also promised that I will never again brush off my husband's opinion without thorough consideration. This was the most costly lesson I have learnt to date, but it was also a turning point in my life.

———————————

I could go on and tell other similar stories of guilt and regret, but the truth is that we are all humans, and it is through making mistakes that we learn. Guilt is not necessarily bad; it is how you cope with it that matters. Many people feel guilty but rather than dealing with the emotion and the causes of the emotion, they go into the ostrich mode and bury their heads in the sand, leaving the negative emotions to stew for years. This is not the answer as it will only attract similar events and experiences into a person's life—because, as you now know; what you focus on expands.

What should you do instead? Accept that you have made a mistake and process the guilt. Learn the lesson you need to learn and promise yourself you won't make the same mistake again. Forgive yourself and love yourself. And if you find it difficult to release your guilty feelings, use the emotion to fuel positive action. Guilt is a highly-charged emotion so turn it into positive energy by using it to take inspired action and make amends for the mistake. Don't let it fester, or it will eat you alive, leading to mental or physical illness. Act quickly to turn your negative emotions into positive ones so your vibrations change, and your life starts to improve as soon as possible.

Emotions: SADNESS AND DEPRESSION
哀和低落

"Simply put, you believe that things or people make you unhappy, but this is not accurate. You make yourself unhappy."

WAYNE DYER

Over the past 10 years, depression has become the main illness in the UK. This is a sad situation. We are all here to enjoy our time on earth because we chose to come for an adventure. But perhaps during the course of this adventure, we have lost sight of our goal. The challenges we face along the way are too much for us, and we have forgotten who we really are. Instead of picking ourselves up, dusting ourselves down and starting again, we lose our will to carry on.

Depression makes us feel as if we have lost control of our lives. It makes us feel victimised, powerless and unable to understand the situation we are in. It usually starts gradually, with feelings of being down and sad. The cause could be grief, due to the loss of a loved one or simply the circumstances of life. Maybe it's simply because we feel misunderstood every day, because an important relationship has broken down or because we have failed at something important to us. Whatever the cause of the low feelings, whether it's fear, blame, disappointment or feeling disempowered, they all contribute to the onset of sadness and depression.

When you are depressed, it is easy to feel trapped by your emotions, causing your world to contract. You feel safe as long as you keep yourself to yourself and keep your emotional door shut. But this only makes things worse as it means you focus on your negative feelings and get sucked deeper and deeper into your own emotional darkness, because as you know by now, what you focus on expands. However, there are a few things that can help you to deal with sadness and depression:

1) Acknowledge that you are feeling sad, depressed, down, disappointed, or whatever else you are feeling. Accept that you are going through a rough patch in life right now.

2) Speak to someone who loves you and cares about you. Usually your gut instinct is to keep everything to yourself and deal with it on your own. You worry that if you tell your parents or loved ones, it will make them worry about you or bring them down too. Wrong! Pushing others away will hurt them more than if you share your feelings. They love you. They can help you and support you. You need them. Speak to them and allow them to help you.

3) Acknowledge that you have lost your momentum, but tell yourself it's just a little hiccup, and it will eventually sort itself out. You can pick up your momentum again simply by changing your thoughts. If you need help with this, you may need to see a professional therapist or counsellor if you don't feel you can talk to your loved ones.

4) Do something different every day to shift yourself out of your routine and comfort zone.

5) Think of something you used to enjoy and do it. Make a decision that you are going to get better every day, and you will take one step at a time to make that happen.

6) Meditation is a great tool to help you and stabilise your emotions. If you don't like to meditate, try visualising yourself being and feeling well again.

I have been through a few difficult patches in my life so I understand how depression feels. I got depressed when I was suspended from work after filing for bankruptcy. I couldn't make sense of my situation. I felt powerless and out of control. I explained to my employer about how the bankruptcy had come about and asked if it would affect my position in the company. I was assured by the human resources officer that it would have no bearing on my employment. But one week later, I was called into a meeting, served the suspension notice and escorted from the building. I wasn't given any explanation. I was shut out by my employer and forbidden to make contact with any of my colleagues. I felt I was being treated like a criminal. I still do not know why I was targeted in this way. I was shocked, embarrassed, humiliated and ashamed. The situation went on for six months before it was resolved, and I was paid some compensation for what happened.

During those six months, I felt confused, lost, angry, frustrated and powerless. I used to stay in bed all day only getting up to do the school run. I walked around the town aimlessly not knowing where to go or even why I was out anyway. Most days, I sat in our spare bedroom just staring into space. I was looking for answers, but I had none and nobody was giving me any. It was the 'not knowing' that got me down.

One morning, when I was aimlessly walking around the house, I spotted a book on the bookcase that I had owned for many years. It caught my eye. It was called *The Power of Your Subconscious Mind*, by Dr Joseph Murphy. I picked it up and started to read it. Things start to shift. My thought patterns changed and my emotions start to lift.

I started to meditate daily any time I felt overwhelmed by my emotions or situation. Each meditation session brought me peace. I decided to do something useful instead of just sitting around the house staring into space. A friend of mine was opening a new café, and she needed help with some renovation work. My friend had asked me to help, but I had said 'no' because I felt so low. I decided to contact my friend and offer her my help. Helping her gave my life some purpose and meaning. It also gave me companionship, conversation and banter that I did not have when I was sitting at home on my own. When I was at the café, I ate lovely food for lunch and enjoyed the company of my friend, who comforted me because she could see I was having a difficult time.

I got out of my depressed state by changing my thought patterns and by taking baby steps. Each day, I did something instead of giving in to my crippling low emotions and my desire to stay in bed all day. If I had allowed myself to stay in that dark place, I probably wouldn't be where I am today.

If you ever find yourself in a dark place, don't give up. Depression is a destructive emotional state, but it can only prevail if we allow it to take us over. You have the power to wipe out your depression by changing your thoughts. Of course, we all need a bit of support at times, and it's important to accept the help you need to get going again. Remember that God loves you unconditionally, and he knocks at your door every day; all you need to do is listen. Your family and friends are rooting for you, so reach out and feel their love and support. They love you very much, whether you believe it or not. The Universe is your biggest ally; all you have to do is ask and be ready to receive. If you know someone who is suffering from depression, please, share this chapter with them. They can change their lives. Tell them not to give up. Life is a gift from God, and it is precious.

Emotions: JOY AND HAPPINESS 喜悅和辛福

"Happiness cannot be travelled to, owned or worn. It is the spiritual experience of living every minute with love, grace and gratitude."

DENNIS WAITLEY

As human beings, happiness is our ultimate goal. This is the emotional place where miracles happen. It is a wonderful feeling, and we naturally want to be immersed in this emotion whenever possible. When was the last time you felt truly joyful and happy? What was the cause of your joy? Was it the birth of a child? Your wedding day? Achieving straight A-grades in your exams? Buying a new car? Moving into your new home? Finding your true love? Winning the lottery? A romantic holiday? A promotion and pay rise at work? Flying first class for the first time ever? A marriage proposal?

Cast your mind back to that moment when you felt joy and happiness. Do you remember the feeling that nothing could upset you when you felt this way? Relive that feeling now. How does it feel? It feels good, doesn't it?

We often associate having money with being happy. But, why do you want money? Is it because of the money itself or because of what you can do with it? Think about this: imagine you got a large amount of money given to you—it can be any amount you wish. What would you do with it?

- Go out for a huge celebration?
- Buy your dream home?
- Buy your dream car?
- Start a business?
- Give money to your family and friends?
- Go on a luxury holiday?
- Donate to the charity of your choice?
- Go and hear your favourite band or singer in concert?

This is why we want money, because it buys us things that make us HAPPY. All these things give you pleasure and it is this that you seek. Why do you want a successful career? So you feel HAPPY and fulfilled. The reason you want what you want is because it makes you happy. And HAPPINESS is your ultimate goal.

Of course, you don't need stuff to be happy. You can feel happy for no reason at all. In fact, you can feel happy and joy every day just by deciding to create that emotion. If you do this, you will feel fulfilled, and all your desires will be manifested easily.

Happiness is also a sign that you have arrived in a good place in your life. All the challenges, hard work and slaying of dragons along the way are now bringing the result you desire. You have made progress, learnt your lessons, overcome hurts and found your way after being lost. You have completed the Hero's Journey and you are now a true hero in your life.

Dear Hannah,

You are special just as you are. Please do not let anyone tell you otherwise. I know you always have trouble making decisions but there are no right or wrong decisions as long as you make decisions based on love and respect for yourself. Have courage and know that every single decision you make will be part of your adventure in time and space.

Stand up for what you believe in. It is a challenging time for your generation, and many of those around you have been sucked into cyberspace by social media. It seems as if everyone is broadcasting news of their life on the internet and it seems as if privacy and respect are non-existent. Some tweets and posts just have 'too much information,' others are downright rude and inappropriate. I hope you are able to decide who to follow, who to accept as friends or followers and who to keep a million miles away from.

Life seems to move with lightning speed, and everything seems to happen in a multi-dimensional way. Everyone is being dragged along in the current of life. Some are running along believing they need to catch up, some are moving so fast that they are struggling to keep their feet on the ground. Others are just drifting and do not know where they are or what they are meant to be. When things are going too fast, and you feel you are drowning, have the courage to step out of the current and let everything flow past you. Stop! Take a look around you, notice what is happening and analyse the situation as best you can. Allow your intuition and emotions to guide you to your rightful place.

Have courage to accept defeat and never get tempted to take on inappropriate challenges. There is no shame in walking away from potential danger, harm or inappropriate behaviour. There is no shame in taking a different path from everyone else.

When times are tough, the path ahead can seem rough and unclear, so when this happens, make sure you ask for help. I love you and will always be there for you. Ask God for direction, accept the Universe as your most powerful ally, listen to your inner guidance and open your arms to receive all the good and gifts from God and the Universe.

Follow your heart, trust your emotions as your guiding system and remember that happiness is your ultimate goal.

Be your true self. Be magnificent. Be a Hero. Always here for you,

Mummy

P.S. By the way, I love your forehead. You are beautiful.

PART TWO

Dear Hannah,

This part of the book is the practical part. It's where you will come when you need help with real life scenarios. I hope that by sharing some of my insights with you in Part Two of this book, you will gain some valuable guidance should you find yourself in similar situations one day.

As I write this book, you are still only 14, so you are preparing for your journey and enjoying a carefree time both at school and at home. This is one of the best periods of your life when everything is new and exciting. There is so much to see and do. You are literally a blank page, ready to be written on, to be added to, to be painted with rainbows, star lights and cow dungs.

There may be many things in this that you find irrelevant when you first read them. You may not understand why or what I am actually talking about at times and you may think, 'My mummy has lost it, I will never do such stupid things!' But sometimes in life, you get sucked into a space where you can't see a way out or you are stuck with a dilemma or in making a decision. You may be forced to make what seem like 'stupid' decisions or decisions you later regret. I do that all the time, even at the grand age of 43. Even today, I said something to a contractor that I wish I hadn't and regretted it immediately. I will apologise to him tomorrow.

I hope Part Two of this book will become a source of wisdom and knowledge for you as you go through life. I hope these chapters will prepare you by giving you an insight into the adventure of creating the life of your dreams. You may think that some of the stories I tell are out of date and will not be relevant to you and your generation.

I thought the same in 2010 when I was given a book called AS A MAN THINKETH, by James Allen. It was written in 1903, and I wondered what I could possibly learn from such an old book? It was not of my generation, and life was different back then. But I was wrong. Every single word and teaching in that book was as relevant to me in 2010 as it was in 1903. Human needs are the same no matter which generation or era they live in. The human race is still experiencing many of the same challenges in 2016 as we did in 1903. In the same way, I know that gong-gong and poh-poh had the same financial and family challenges back in 1970s and 80s as we do now. Some things never change.

Since reading James Allen's book, I have read many others that come from a different era. They include: THE SCIENCE OF GETTING RICH by Wallace B Wattles, which was written in 1900. Napoleon Hill's book THINK AND GROW RICH was written in 1937. THE SILVA METHOD by Jose Silva was published in 1966. THE SKY'S THE LIMIT by Wayne Dyer was written in 1980 and AWAKEN THE GIANT WITHIN by Tony Robbins was written in 1991.

All these books are about the power of the mind and universal and timeless human needs and problems. Each author offers tools and techniques to help solve money problems, relationship issues and health challenges. They help readers achieve success, true happiness and promote well-being. I cannot predict the future but based on historical evidence and trends, I am confident that the next few generations will behave and think like those who are living now and who have lived since 1900 and before. So in many ways the future will be much the same as it is now.

Love Mummy

CHAPTER FIVE
Education and School Life

YOUR SCHOOL LIFE and education are important times in your life. This is the time when you learn about yourself, find out about your personality, develop your intellectual and life skills and enjoy new experiences every day. Are you in education at the moment? Do you like school? Do you enjoy college? Are you thriving at university? Or are you stressing about your PhD dissertation?

When we are at school, most of us have our favourite subjects and teachers. We are also not so keen on certain subjects and dislike certain teachers. We even give our teachers nicknames for fun. It is fair to say that we usually do well at the subjects we like, and we tend not to perform so well at subjects we are not so keen on. Which of these following statements do you think is true?

A: You are not doing so well at a particular subject and not getting good grades because you don't like studying it.

B: You tried hard at a particular subject but didn't get the result you wanted so now you dislike studying it.

The answer I usually get at my workshops is B.

At the workshops I run for students aged 12 to 18, the students confirmed that they had lost interest in a subject after they tried hard at it but didn't get the results they were hoping for. When they kept getting disappointed, they created a story to justify the situation, and the story they made up was that they did not like the subject so they were not interested in succeeding in it. But the truth is that once the story about not liking a subject was firmly registered in their subconscious mind, they were programmed to get the same result every time: failure.

In order to change the result, those young people needed to change their thinking and beliefs. It's the same for us all. When things aren't going well, we need to tell ourselves a different story. If you have tried many times to pass an exam and still did not get the grades you wanted, you need to take a new approach to learning. You need to get help from a different teacher because a different teacher may be able to explain a topic better than the one you have now. You need to read different text-books and other resources because they may explain things in a better way for you. Have you looked into the possibility of getting private tuition or additional training? Have you thought about hiring a coach or mentor to help you?

If things aren't going well, tell yourself a different story: "I am good at science. I am open and receptive to new ways of learning and understanding the subject. I have excellent grades." Never give up. The human brain is the most powerful tool in the entire galaxy. It has the potential to learn and create almost anything. Do not give your power away by telling stories that do not support your goals and aspirations.

❀ *My Story*

I was not happy for the whole of the first three years of my primary school (that's the same as junior school in the UK). I believed I was stupid and so my whole experience was that of feeling stupid. As I have told you, I came from Chinese village in Malaysia. But what I haven't told you before is that although I can speak Bahasa Malaysia, the national language, my first language is Cantonese. English is foreign language which is part of our curriculum and a compulsory subject. I did not understand a single word of English when I started junior school. I really struggled with it as my brain wasn't wired to understand such a peculiar language. I hated learning English, and I was scared of it.

My favourite cousin, Sow Kheng, is five years older than me so she offered to help me with my English. I remembered clearly how upset she was after she sat with me for a whole day trying to teach me how to read 'eye', 'ear', 'nose', 'mouth' and 'hair'. Not only was I not able to pronounce the words properly, I couldn't remember which word corresponded with each part of my face. After three hours, she went off in tears.

I felt terrible, and I was annoyed with myself for being so stupid! I loved my cousin very much, and she was everything I wanted to be at the time. She was beautiful, she played the piano and she spoke English. She was the only person who seemed to care about me so I felt very guilty about upsetting her. In that moment, I made a promise to myself to become very good at English so I could prove to her that I'm not stupid. Sow Kheng was the only one of my cousins who never called me 'fat girl' or made fun of me. She has always been very kind to me, and she is still my favourite cousin today.

Writing this book is evidence that I kept my promise. I didn't know it at the time, but when I made that promise, I made a commitment to change. I altered my thinking and beliefs. I created a new story for myself; the past was history. All I remember is that from that moment forward, I did well at English. When I was fifteen, I was one of the top students in the senior school in English. That one tiny decision changed my life.

Social Life

"When you are content to simply be yourself and don't compare or compete with others, everybody will respect you."

LAO TZE

Friends play a big part in our lives. We all have our favourite and our not so favourite friends. When I was at school, I had a friend called Melissa. I remember that one day we were friends and the next day we weren't. A few days later, we were friends again. The cycle is the same for many school friendships, and it was the same for me and my peer group.

I was not a popular girl at school. I was ordinary. I had a couple of friends I played with every day. There are always girls and boys who belong to the popular group, and they attract attention wherever they go and by doing whatever they do. They are like celebrities at school. Everyone knows them. Some of us despise them and some of us will do anything to get in with them. Usually, but not always, these girls and boys are popular purely because of their good looks and charm.

At the other end of the spectrum, there are those who are academically bright but do not pay much attention to their appearance. They are usually the teachers' favourites but are not very popular with the other pupils. Then there are boys and girls like me—and maybe like you—who are not popular and believe that they are not good at many things. They have a couple of friends at school but not many. They look at the popular girls and boys and, sometimes, they envy them because of the attention they get. Sometimes, they wish they could be part of their group. They wonder if their lives would be more exciting if they were friends with those popular people, but at other times they just don't bother about them.

As I said at the very beginning of this book, each and every one of us is special. Each of us has our own unique qualities, DNA and personalities. Some of our friends are a good match for our personalities and some are not. We cannot force anyone to be our friend, and we cannot manipulate anyone to like us or do anything that they don't want to do. Likewise, no one can make us happy unless we are happy in ourselves. Let's look at these ideas in a bit more detail.

When you meet someone at school or anywhere, why are you attracted to that person and try to become friends? Is it because he or she is:

- Funny?
- Always smiling and happy?
- Confident?
- Top of the class in maths or science?
- Captain of a sports team?
- Kind and caring?
- Beautiful and attractive?
- Handsome and good looking?
- Polite?
- Honest?
- Cool?

Or, are you attracted to this person because he or she is:
- Temperamental?
- Boastful?
- Miserable?
- Timid?
- Sly?
- Bottom of the class in most of subjects?
- Lacks confidence?

- Unkind?
- Uncaring?
- Gossips all the time?
- Tell lies about other people?

The first group of people who are funny, confident and kind are examples of happy people. This group does not rely on those around them to make them happy. In fact, they are the ones who bring happiness and joy to others. That is why people are attracted to them. The second group are the ones who are likely to sit on their own at lunchtime, and who may not have many friends either in or out of school. They often try hard to impress others hoping they will become friends with them. They frequently seem hurt or disappointed about things and tend to perceive the world as unfair. They probably feel resentful towards the people in the first group. If you want to change your life, start with yourself because if you change your thoughts and beliefs about yourself, your experience of the world will change too.

✸ *Felicity's Story*

Felicity was 12 years old when her mother, Bernice, asked me for help. Felicity was struggling at school in every area: academic, sport and social. Also, Bernice has received various complaints from the school and other parents regarding Felicity's behaviour. Felicity had been causing trouble amongst her school friends from the first day she went to school, and she had problems making friends. She was never invited to birthday parties or to play days. Bernice would invite Felicity's friends over in an attempt to bridge the gap and foster friendship between her daughter and the other children. She hoped that the children would invite Felicity back in return, but it never happened. Things got worse when Bernice finally found out the truth from the school and other parents.

Grace was one of the popular girls at school and Felicity was very fond of Grace. Felicity would follow Grace everywhere during break and lunch times. But when other children tried to speak to Grace or play with her, Felicity would become unpleasant. She dragged Grace away from others by force. If the other children persisted in trying to spend time with Grace, Felicity made rude and unkind remarks to them so she could make them go away. Grace would come up with excuses to get away from her, but Felicity would follow Grace everywhere. She would even stand outside the toilet and waited for Grace if she had to.

Felicity had also tried to manipulate Bernice on one occasion. She told her mother that she was being bullied at school by the girls who tried to take Grace away from her. Not knowing any better, Bernice went to the school thinking she was protecting her child. However, when she got to the school, Bernice discovered that there had recently been an incident where Felicity had intentionally flooded the girls' toilets in an attempt to get one of Grace's best friends into trouble.

Felicity was trying too hard to befriend Grace, and she was going about it the wrong way. In fact, everything Felicity did only succeeded in pushing both Grace and everyone else away. Felicity couldn't understand why nobody liked her. Despite all the trouble she caused, Felicity couldn't do enough for Grace, but this just made her even more suffocating.

I worked with Felicity for three sessions. In our first session, Felicity learnt to love and accept herself just as she is. She learnt that she cannot manipulate or force someone to do anything that they do not want to do. If you could not like or love yourself, no one can. She discovered that she couldn't win friends by hurting others. After this, Felicity changed her thinking and instead of going to school feeling worried that the entire school disliked her, she started to visualise herself being happy and walking confidently into school with a smile on her face. She focused on all the fun things she would be doing during the day rather than what she was going to do to monopolise her best friends' time during break and lunch.

When Felicity came back for her second session three weeks later, her posture and appearance had completely changed. She was happy and confident. Bernice looked relieved and pleased. Felicity reported that she had made some new friends; friends she had never noticed before because she was too busy concentrating on Grace. She noticed that she didn't need to do anything to attract her new friends—they came to her, she didn't have to chase them. Felicity was surprised about how well she and her new friends got along. It was as if they had known each other for years. In fact, one of the girls had already invited Felicity for a sleepover on Friday night. Felicity was thrilled. In the second session, we worked on affirmations to ensure that the new thought patterns and beliefs were established in her mind. In our third and final session, we also looked at meditation. This was a tool that helped Felicity get centred again when things were tough.

Three months ago, I contacted Bernice to ask her permission to include Felicity's case in this book. She said 'yes' and also gave me an update on Felicity's progress. It turns out that since our sessions, Felicity has also improved her academic results. Felicity is now a happy teenager.

❋ Charlie's Story

Charlie was invited out by a popular group of kids from school. They were going ice-skating. He was delighted and thrilled. His parents dropped him at the venue, and he met up with the group. It was a privilege to be a part of that group so he was very happy. Half an hour later, his parents got a call from Charlie asking them to pick him up from the rink.

They went to pick him up and asked Charlie what was wrong as they weren't expecting him home until later in the day as the boys were supposed to be having dinner after the ice skating. Charlie said, "I don't want to be part of what they do. They were bullying young children at the ice rink. If being popular means doing things like that, I don't want to be part of it."

Much of the time, things are not what they seem. You may like someone, but this someone may not be a good fit for your personality. If you force the situation, things would be unnatural; out of synch. Sometimes, when you get to know the popular girls or boys, they may not be the people you think they are, and you may be disappointed.

The truth is that we are not designed to get along with everyone, which means we are not meant to be best friends with everybody. If you spend all your time trying to 'fit in' just because you want to please someone you like, you will lose the chance to learn how to be yourself. That means nobody will have a chance to get to know the real you.

God and the Universe are always providing for us. They care not only our physical and material needs but also our emotional and spiritual needs. Enjoy your time at school and college. Don't get too hung up on being friends with certain people or groups. Trust God and the Universe that your needs will be met. All the friends you need are around you, and it is up to you to reach out and accept them into your life with joy and gratitude.

Be yourself. "Be YOU. You are SPECIAL and MAGNIFICENT, so let the world get to know the real YOU.

CHAPTER SIX
Career and Work Life

The only way to do great work is to love what you do. If you haven't found it yet, keep looking. Don't settle.

STEVE JOBS

Follow your passion

When you're at school, you're always being asked what you want to do when you grow up. This seems to imply that you are expected to say you want to be an architect, a teacher, a soldier, a bus driver, a pilot, a doctor, or something similar. The implication is that you need to finish your education so you can get a job. There is nothing wrong with that, but I feel that this means you are being asked to make one of the most important decisions in your life without any proper guidance or understanding. Nine out of ten of the students I coached in my workshop had the same idea of what lay ahead of them: complete their education, get a job, start a family, work in a job for the rest of their lives until retirement age, go on a holiday once or twice a year, buy a car, buy a house, maybe move a few times and settle in one final property for their retirement.

They did not know any other way because this was how they had been programmed to think by their families. I found this very frightening and disturbing. We are supposed to be the most intelligent species on earth and yet we are nothing but drones. It's as if we're run by computer programmes. We have lost our individuality and forgotten what our passion is in life. We let society, politicians and our environment rob us of our gifts and bury them under the piles of bills, laundry, work that doesn't excite us, debt, stress and whatever else is dumped on us simply because this is the only life we believe is available to us.

"What is your passion?" is a much more appropriate question to ask our children when they are at school. The question, "What do you enjoy doing even when you are doing it for free?" will get a much more meaningful answer from children than, "What do you want to do when you leave school." Asking someone what they enjoy sparks their imagination and the free flow of energy. When I asked the same question about passion at my workshop, I received happy, excited answers. I saw the children's eyes sparkle, the conversation start to flow and the room filled with energy and joy! It was amazing to feel the passion and excitement.

It is a completely different reaction to the question: "What do you want to be when you grow up?" The answers I got to this question were rehearsed. It felt like an obligation to say something 'clever' that their parents would be proud of. There was very little passion from most of the children when they answered that question. There was no excitement. The conversation stopped after the answer was shared. No one felt that they needed to say anymore. No one felt that they had anything else to add.

❀ My Story

I have been a building surveyor for over 15 years. It has been my career. When I put on my safety boots and walk onto a construction site with my hard hat on, I often wonder how on earth I got myself into this job. I am usually the only woman on site. Great, I have proved a point. But who am I proving it to? The people on site? My dear departed grandma? My auntie who lost her battle with cancer? Or is it just to myself? The truth is no one cares whether I am a building surveyor or a woman doing a man's job. The decision I made when I was 15, does not matter anymore. All the people I want to prove wrong when I chose to be a building surveyor are no longer alive to see me! Is it worth it? I enjoy what I do, but it is not where my passion lies.

When I was 15, Papa asked me what I wanted to do when I left school. He suggested that I train to become a teacher. He said being a teacher is a good job, and it is a safe job. I told Papa that I could not survive on a teacher's salary. I want much more than just a mediocre life. I also thought (wrongly) that teaching was a women's job, and I didn't want to do a women's job. I needed to prove to my grandma and auntie that I am capable of doing a man's job. I may not be a man, but I am as clever and as capable, if not better than men. I wanted to prove them wrong. So, Papa's suggestion was scrapped, and the idea of a building surveyor was born.

What is my passion? I wish someone had asked me this question when I was a teenager. I am passionate about helping people to improve their lives. When I see beggars on the street, my heart goes out to them. I wish I could provide them with shelter, food and a way to help them to get back on their feet. When I see orphans begging, I wish I could provide them with a home and education and give them a second chance in life so they can see that things can be different.

When I was 18 and still living in Malaysia, my best friend, Chee Fung, asked me, "What is your dream?" Without a second thought, I said I wanted to make lot of money so that I could open an orphanage for children who lived on the street and a shelter for beggars. I did not want to see anyone living on the streets in Malaysia. This is still my dream and my passion. When I was 18, it was only a dream or aspiration. Today, I have a mission. I have details and clarity on what I really want to do.

I not only want to start an orphanage I want to give those children the opportunity to improve themselves, to change their limiting beliefs, to help them to find their passion and create a meaningful and fulfilling life in the future. It is also my passion to help homeless people get back on their feet and start a new life. I am not interested in giving them money, but I would like to provide shelter, a temporary home, food and training to help them get a job and start over. It is not about getting them off the street temporarily but getting them off the street for good so they can find their passion and create a meaningful and fulfilling life. Writing this book is the start of my mission. I want to give anyone who will listen a basic understanding of how the power and magic of life works, starting with my lovely daughter, Hannah

———————————

Take out your journal and answer these questions:

- What is your passion? What is the one thing you would do even if you were not being paid to do it?
- Are you in job that excites you?
- Are you in your job just for the money?

- Do you feel fulfilled at work?
- Do you feel you are stuck in the rat race?
- Are you happy with your current job?
- What stops you from pursuing your passion?
- If you won the lottery, what would you do? Of course, you will go out and celebrate, buy your dream house, your dream cars, give away some money to your family, friends and charities, go on luxury holidays, etc. But once the excitement has died down and the dust has settled, what would you do?

Once you have given your answers to these questions, think about how you could start to live your passion. Take baby steps. It is time to plan and take action.

"Here's to the crazy ones. The misfits. The rebels. The trouble-makers. The round pegs in the square holes–. The ones who see things differently– They're not fond of rules And they have no respect for the status quo– You can quote them, disagree with them, glorify or vilify them. About the only thing you can't do is ignore them because they change things. They push the human race forward. And while some may see them as crazy ones, we see genius. Because the people who are crazy enough to think they can change the world, are the ones who do."

ROB SILTANEN

Starting Your Own Business

You may decide you want to start your own business or become an entrepreneur rather than getting a job or training for a career. You may choose to start a business on your own or with a friend or family member. If you choose to create a partnership with someone you know, you must be willing and able to separate your personal relationship from your business one.

If you decide you would like to take this alternative work route, I would like to offer you a few pointers to help you on your way. This is advice that I wish someone had given me before I embarked on my own business venture. I would have had fewer bruises to my confidence, jumped through a few less hoops and got started faster if I'd had this kind of help when I was starting out. Here's what I have learnt and I hope it will help you in starting your own business.

1) It is crucial that you know what you are passionate about before you begin. What are you setting out to achieve? How are you going to turn your passion into a career, income or a business?

"No man can succeed in a line of endeavor he does not like."

NAPOLEON HILL

---

2) An entrepreneur is someone who supplies the solution to a problem being experienced by a specific group of people or fulfils their need for something. Create a business that sells or produces a product or service that an identifiable group of people want. Whatever you do, you must fulfil a need, provide entertainment or pleasure or offer a solution to a specific problem. Make sure that group is one you can find and that it is large enough to sustain your business.

3) Every time you hear 'no' you get another step closer to a 'yes'. In other words, make it your goal to fail as many times as possible and as fast as you can because that means success is getting closer.

"Develop success from failures. Discouragement and failure are two of the surest stepping stones to success."

DALE CARNEGIE

---

4) Work out your minimum cost of living so you will be able to pay your bills and look after yourself and your family (if you have a family). Knowing your numbers will help you work out your prices and the minimum number of sales you need to make each week or month. After that, treat everything else as if it's a bonus. This will reduce your anxiety and stress.

5) Run your business with compassion and love. Keep your word. Offer your clients what you would like to be offered yourself. If you do not like being treated a certain way, it's probable that your clients won't like it either.

6) Hire an accountant from day one or preferably before you start your business. A good accountant will save you money and help you deal with tax in a legal and appropriate way. This is priceless when managing the financial side of your business in the long term.

Go on, have a go. Success is waiting for you and all you have to do is take inspired action with faith and passion. Act as if you are the person you want to become and everything else will fall into place.

Why Keeping Your Word Matters

In 2014, my friend and I organised a three-day Spa and Retreat event. One of the attendees of the spa event, Tracy, paid a deposit as well as two further instalments towards the cost of the event. However, two weeks before the event, Tracy contacted us to ask for a refund explaining that she had been diagnosed with cancer and only had two months to live.

When our clients paid their deposit, they also signed an agreement acknowledging that the deposit would become non-refundable a month before the event. It was also clear that only a certain percentage of the money would be refunded in the event of cancellation. Our rules stated that no money would be refunded two weeks before the event.

But as our business purpose and passion was around helping others and improving lives, we decided to refund Tracy's money in full. Even though we were legally within our rights to refuse, we decided we couldn't do that because it would have gone against our core beliefs and the fundamental reason behind what we set out to do with our work.

Tracy may or may not have been telling the truth but that didn't matter. What mattered was our conscience. This shows how important it is that you don't violate the law of the Universe and God's law of unconditional love. I remembered Papa saying, "Never take advantage of dying people; in fact, give them whatever you can to help them. Love them and care for them and hopefully in doing so, they can pass over with love and peace."

Papa also explained if the person who died held a grudge against us, we would have a difficult time ahead. He was not saying that the person's ghost would come back to haunt us; it is more about our own beliefs and staying true to who we are. It is in everybody's best interest to make peace with the dying. In fact, make peace with the living. Forgive, let go and let God.

Dying or not, if someone changes their mind about an event or a product, don't hold it against them and don't try to hold on to them. Refund the money and let them go. They're probably not ready, or they may be short of money and by letting them go, you have created a positive experience for them, gained their trust or even have their blessing. If you hold on to the money, they are likely to feel annoyed and the next thing you know, you will have created negative vibes around them. Added to that, they are unlikely to say anything positive about you and your business and that can only harm you both.

CHAPTER SEVEN
Money and Prosperity
錢 不 是 萬 能 · 沒 錢 就 萬 萬 不 能

"Empty pockets never held anyone back. Only empty heads and empty hearts can do that."

NORMAN VINCENT PEALE

Relationship with Money

- I don't have enough money for holidays.
- I can't afford that beautiful handbag.
- I am always struggling to make ends meet.
- I am stressed because I know I don't have enough money to cover my direct debits next week.
- Flying Business Class can only ever be a dream.
- I don't have a degree so I will never earn £50,000 a year.
- I am anxious about paying the school fees.
- I have so much debt I don't know what to do.
- I mustn't buy meat because I am really struggling with money this month.
- How will I ever be able to get to work this week? I don't have any money for fuel.
- I only have 50 pence left! I can't even afford a box of eggs for dinner tonight.

The list is a summary of the kind of things I was saying about my financial situation for years. It was my money story. By reading it, you can probably guess what sort of life I was leading in those days! It was a life of lack, anxiety, worry, stress, fear, frustration, guilt and chaos. Every day, I woke up feeling frightened and anxious, worrying how I would be able to get through the day or week. It was always one thing on top of another and with each negative event, I ended up spending money I didn't have. The car broke down so I got stressed. The Council Tax was due, and I knew I didn't have the money to pay the direct debit. I paid for a holiday but had to cancel it because I didn't have any spending money.

I was stuck in this pattern of thinking around money for years and, as a result, I got very angry and frustrated with myself and my life. Every January, April and September, I have to pay Hannah's school fees. Every time, in the weeks leading up to the date when the school fees were due, I would become stressed because, no matter what I did, I was always in the position where I had to scrape together every single penny to make up the school fees. It made no difference what I was earning (at one point, I was earning £8,000 a month), when it came to paying the school fees, I never had the money. Eventually, I realised that this problem kept recurring regardless of how much I was earning because the problem wasn't the money I had coming in, it was about my money beliefs—beliefs I had been nurturing unconsciously for many years.

I believe that a good education is the most important foundation any child can have, and I wanted to give Hannah the best education I could, whether I was able to afford it or not. I believed that the best education is a private education but I also believed that a private education is expensive and that I can't afford it. I am a stubborn person, and I was determined to give Hannah the best education possible, whether I could afford it or not. So, from the day Hannah first started reception school, I manifested every doubt and drama I had around the decision to pay for her (expensive) education. Somehow, I always managed to get the fees together, but only with a lot of stress and struggle. The school fees were paid mostly on time, sometimes they were a little late, but Hannah was getting the best possible education and, that was all that mattered.

However, I then realised that I was playing a mind-movie over and over again, and this was not supportive of finding the school fees with ease. This is the movie I ran in my mind around the school fees: the movie reveals a worn out mother, looking frail but feeling proud and giving everything to provide the best for her daughter. Everyone admires her for her love and sacrifice but watches her struggle to come up with the school fees. The entire audience are touched by her actions and love for her daughter. The mother has a sense of achievement; she is proud that she is able to find the money all by herself. She hopes her daughter will know how much she has done for her and love her for her efforts and sacrifice.

This movie was so engrained in my subconscious mind that I no longer noticed it existed. Each time the school fee event came around, my subconscious would play the movie automatically, over and over again; thereby, manifesting the feelings engendered by the movie each time. The only flaw with the movie and the manifestation was there were no audience. I did not get the applause or sympathy that I was craving by running my mind movie. I did not get the recognition I wanted as a selfless mother because the only audience I had was me!

Everything that happened had taken place in my head first. I had created all the struggle, stress, drama and lack because that movie had been playing in my head over and over again. This movie had been projected onto my silver screen of life, just for my benefit! In other words, it was my fault that I was struggling with the fees because I wanted it to be that way. I was craving approval, love and sympathy through the drama I created. The truth hit me like a meteor and made me feel sick. The impact is beyond what I could comprehend. How wrong could my perceptions be?

What movie are you running in your mind? Do you have an unconscious desire that is creating your reality? Is there a deep-seated feeling that is causing you to struggle and experience lack in your life? Have you ever felt that you are stuck in a cycle that doesn't serve you? If so, search for it, erase it and start a new movie!

The Chinese say, "Money is not invincible but without money, nothing is possible." Money is energy, and energy needs to flow in order for it to reach its full potential. Energy is expressed as a vibration, and your personal vibration is influenced by your thoughts and emotions. What is your relationship with money? As you can see from my mind movie, my relationship with money is one of conflict. I want money, but I am also using money or portraying money as the 'bad guy' in my life so I can be the 'good guy'. I'm showing 'my world' that it was because of 'lack of money' that I struggled and led a stressful life.

I was being unfair to money, and I was never going to create a good relationship with it if all I was concerned about was making myself look good by making money look bad. After all, how would you feel if one day you found out that your partner had been telling everyone that you were horrible and unreasonable just so they could be seen as the 'good guy'? What would you do if you had to be the 'bad guy' all the time? You'd feel hurt and angry, right? You might even leave the relationship. You'd probably fight or ignore your partner for months. You wouldn't want to talk things through or work on building a harmonious relationship, would you?

Your relationship with money is the same. If you want money in your life, you have to love and respect it. You need to be grateful for the money you have. I wasn't grateful; I was ungrateful, and I expressed my disrespect and lack of gratitude with my thoughts and my internal movie. That was why money never wanted to stay with me. I was in debt, struggling to find the school fees, stressed over unpaid bills and finding it hard to make ends meet because I was disregarding how much money I earned. I had gone from earning £1,600 a month to £8,000 a month within 18 months, but my financial situation didn't improve much.

You probably tell yourself and others that you love money, but how do you love money? Do you love it because of what it can buy or bring you? Many of us think money brings us happiness. We depend on money. We worship money. Money pulls at our heart strings and creates powerful emotions. Money comes first. But this is not love. It is more of an obsession. Here are a few suggestions on how to improve your relationship with money:

- Treat your money with love and respect as you would a precious friend.
- Be generous with your money but not wasteful.
- Spend it joyously and gratefully, trust that it will return to you. When your partner or family members go out, do you doubt or worry that they won't return? Money likes to be circulated. Spend joyously and wisely, and money will come back to you a thousand times over.
- Pay all your bills with a grateful heart. After all, a service has been rendered in exchange for your money. Be grateful for your mobile phone, your home, your car, the electricity, gas, rubbish collection services and everything else that money buys for you. Appreciate money as the tool that delivers you a good quality of life. Never take this for granted.
- Be practical and learn to manage money wisely. This will prepare your path to better financial position in the future. Everyone,

including the multi-millionaires, needs to know how to manage money effectively and wisely.

- Use money only for good. When you use money for good, you create energised thoughts and emotions, emitting high vibrations that will attract abundance from the Universe. Use it for evil or fraud, and your vibration will block abundance from reaching you. The vibration that comes from evil is not a match with the good vibrations from the Universe.

- Respect and rejoice in the wealth and success enjoyed by other.

- Use money purposefully. Have you discovered your passion? Take inspired action and follow your passion because money is attracted to those with purpose who also take action with passion.

Now that you understand your relationship with money, let's go a one step further and start to create your money blueprint and money story. As I briefly mentioned in earlier chapters of this book, each of us has a blueprint for our life which is imprinted within our personal belief system. This blueprint clearly set out the expectations we have for our lives.

What type of money stories do you tell your friends and family? What type of money stories do you tell yourself in the quiet of the night? What sort of emotions do your money stories conjure up for you? What is your money blueprint, and what are your money beliefs? At the beginning of this chapter, I shared with you some of my own money stories and beliefs. Below is a summary of my blueprint about money:

- My earnings are capped at £32,000 a year gross because I do not have a degree—I can't earn more than this.

- I do not have any savings because I do not have enough money to make ends meet.

- I can afford to eat out every week if I want to because I love eating out, and I can afford it.

So, up until three years ago, I had never earned more than £32,000 a year, in fact, sometimes I earned even less than this. I believed I couldn't earn more than this sum because I didn't have a degree. I didn't believe anyone would give me a job at higher salary because of my lack of a degree. I believed that if I was offered a job where I earn more than £32,000 a year, I would lose it within a short period of time. I also failed to save any money. Each time I managed to save, I would sabotage myself by unconsciously creating a situation that required me to dip into my savings. Any money I amassed was often gone in no time. I loved eating out so I convinced myself that I could always afford to eat out (even if I couldn't actually afford it in reality). This was my money blueprint. I had an unwritten set of rules built into my blueprint that said:

- I should own a house by now.
- I should have good investments and savings by now.
- I should be able to afford what I want in life by now.
- I should be earning more money and have a management-level role by now.

The only problem was that this second set of rules contradicts the first set of rules. But why did the first set of rules manifest itself in my life and not the second? It was because my beliefs and emotions are much stronger around the first set of rules. The first set of rules dominated my thinking and created the powerful emotions of fear and worry. I focused on these thoughts and emotions every day. They were always there at the back of my mind because I didn't pay attention to my thoughts and modify them.

The second set of rules only engendered lukewarm emotions. I believed they were true but they didn't resonate with my core being. The word 'should' is a give-away and indicates that something I was regurgitating something because I was told it was right and what I 'should' have wanted. It wasn't my idea. It was society's idea or my family's or part of my culture's expectations.

Before I understand how all the energy of the Universe worked, I used to get upset with myself and disappointed that I wasn't delivering or achieving what I thought I 'should'. I felt useless, and I felt I had let my parents down. I felt I was not good enough. With these thoughts going through my mind, you can imagine the type of emotional home I was living in; it was a home that supported my first set of rules about not having a degree so not being good enough to earn more money or not having enough money to open a savings account. It was stuck in a vicious circle.

Make Your Money Stories Work for You

Have you noticed that we're all excellent story tellers? I now understand that it was not the money but my mindset and attitude towards money that was causing the problems with my finances. For example, when I kept telling myself the story of how I never had enough money to make ends meet so I couldn't afford to open a savings account, I was lying to myself. The truth was that I didn't want to open a savings account. I didn't believe it was important. When I was challenged on this, I came up with a legitimate money story that prevented me from saving, namely that I couldn't make ends meet so I couldn't start saving.

What's interesting is that, even though I couldn't afford to save, I could always afford to go out for a meal. That's because eating out was what I really wanted to do. I could always justify spending money on going out for a meal because that was what I wanted to do. In truth, I could have cut down on the amount of eating out I did and put the money into a savings account, but that wasn't what I wanted to do, so I didn't.

Ask yourself what stories you're making up to justify you doing what you want to do and stopping you doing what you need to do. Study those stories. Make a list of them then look at them and decide if you are going to keep these stories or start creating different and more supportive stories.

Next, take a look at some common stories or beliefs you may be telling yourself so you can decide whether they are serving you or whether you want to change them.

Money story 1: "I am too young to get rich." or "I am too old to get rich."

Please do not fall into the same trap that I did. Age has nothing to do with getting rich or making a fortune. It is just a number. Mark Zuckerberg, the founder of Facebook, made his first million dollars when he was at college. Madison Nicole Robinson created FishFlops when she was twelve and earned $1 million in sales before she could drive. Fraser Doherty, a Scottish Entrepreneur, set up SuperJam when he was 14 years old using his grandma's recipes. SuperJam now supplies over 2,000 supermarkets and Fraser is now a millionaire. The late Tan Sri Dato Seri Lim Goh Tong, the founder of Genting Group, made his first million when he was over 50. Age is not the issue, your beliefs and money stories are.

Money story 2: "I do not have a good enough education so I can't be successful." or "I do not have a degree so I can't be a success."

There are so many millionaires and billionaires who have very little education. They don't have certificates of any kind, let alone a degree. Andrew Carnegie, Henry Ford, Bill Gates, Richard Branson, Simon Cowell are just a few people who have made it without being university or college educated.

Money story 3: "Money is the root of all evil."

Money is just a tool and a tool cannot be evil. It is the user who makes the tool evil or good. It is you or me who choose how to use money. We can use it for good, or we can choose to use it for evil. It is the love of money that is the root of all evil, not money itself. Money is neutral.

Money story 4: "Wealthy people are stingy and unkind."

My grandma always says, "One type of rice feeds a hundred types of people." There are stingy and unkind people everywhere, not just those who are wealthy or rich. Even if you meet some unkind wealthy people, this does not mean you are going to be the same as them when you are rich. It is your choice whether you are a kind and generous wealthy person or a stingy and unkind wealthy person. In fact, I have the privilege to meet many wealthy people who are both generous and kind. It is your choice. Come on, have the courage, claim your wealth from The Universe. Prove this to the world that you are a kind, loving and generous wealthy person!

Money story 5: "It is unholy or unspiritual to desire wealth."

Where do you get this from? The Bible? Buddhism? Wherever this idea comes from, it is not from God. God wants the best for us. God created humankind to enjoy the earth. If you know your Bible, you will know that Abraham, Moses, Ruth and Job were all millionaires in their time. They are God fearing characters who are spiritual as well as Biblical heroes. Prosperity is at the heart of Buddhism. Everything Buddhists practise includes rituals for attracting wealth, money, health and prosperity. The Chinese even go to the extent of giving prosperous names to the dishes they eat every day especially celebratory dishes during Chinese New Year. Wealthy people are more spiritual as they do not have to focus on their own needs or worry about how they are going to pay the next bill.

Wealthy people are able to focus on contributing and supporting others. Wealth and spirituality go hand in hand.

Money story 6: "You cannot get rich doing what you love."

Really? Look around you. Look on the internet. Look everywhere. What do you see? Compare the work that rich people do with the work that so-called 'ordinary' people do. Rich people make their money by following their passions and doing what they love. 'Ordinary' people often lead mediocre lives or lives where they experience lack and stress. They are usually working flat out because they are stuck in the rat race, struggling to make ends meet and doing jobs they hate. They're putting up with colleagues or bosses they can't bear. Do you need any more evidence to convince you that doing what you love is a sure-fire way to get rich? Bear Grylls does what he loves. Who would have thought that his love of the outdoors, adventure and survival would have brought him so much success and fame? Steven Spielberg never gave up on his passion to be a movie director; he is one of the best and most well-respected directors in the world.

It is time for you to do some work. Take out your journal and write down all your beliefs and money stories putting each one on a separate page. Write out your story or belief, then cross it out and write a new story underneath it. You can use facts or stories, but whatever you write must replace the old belief. Do it now. Put this book down and do it now. Come back to the book when you're finished.

"Money is only a tool. It will take you wherever you wish, but it will not replace you as the driver."

AYN RAND

What is Your Money Goal?

One of the most common stories I hear when I run my seminars is that people are unhappy in their work because they are not paid enough, or because the company they work for doesn't appreciate them. Kerry works for an organisation in Reading. She has been there for over 18 years. Two years ago, there was a corporate restructure and everyone's job was re-graded. Kerry was amongst the few who had their pay frozen for 12 months before it was reduced to fit a lower pay grade. Kerry was unhappy with the situation, and she felt stuck and frustrated. When her pay was reduced, she had very little left at the end of the month after paying her bills.

Despite this, Kerry was undecided about leaving her job because she felt the company should appreciate her as a conscientious worker, a loyal employee, and because of her love for the company. Kerry became very bitter about the entire situation. When Kerry came to my workshop, I asked her to tell me her goal from this situation. What outcome did she want to see? She said she wanted her employer to appreciate her and return her to her old pay grade. I have been in a very similar situation to Kerry, as had many of the other delegates at the workshop, but here is the truth about this situation:

1) You cannot control either an individual's or a company's decisions or actions.
2) You cannot force a person, company or event to change to suit your wishes.

What Kerry—and indeed most of us in that situation—want is to control or influence the situation. In this case, make the company change their mind about their pay grades so we get what we want. God and the Universe do not force anything on anyone unless there is a mutual agreement or vibrational match. If you are like me, your goal will be to earn the money you want to earn. It doesn't matter whether I work for company A or company B. That is not part of my goal. The job title doesn't matter to me. It's the end result of earning £40,000 a year that matters and working close to home or from home.

Kerry decided that money was her goal, and after a long discussion around her expectations in relation to her current company, it became apparent that she felt a strong connection to the company, so she felt hurt and disappointed by the way she had been treated. I believe this is common for many employees around the world

When I talked about loving yourself earlier in this book, this is one of the situations where you need to work on loving yourself more. Loving yourself involves appreciating YOURSELF; loving yourself and accepting yourself just as you are. YOU want to get to a point where you don't need others to show your appreciation and love in order for you to feel happy. When you need appreciation from others in order to love yourself, you are giving away your own happiness because your happiness depends on your expectation of appreciation from others. Never give away your power and remember that happiness comes from within. You are special and magnificent. You do not need others to tell you so.

Kerry got a new job that paid her more than she had earned on her old grade. The new company had the added benefit of being only a five minute walk from home instead of a 30-minute drive. One of Kerry's fears around getting a new job had been around her lack of qualifications. She thought she wouldn't get another job at all, let alone one that exceeded her salary in her old company.

Are you in similar situation to Kerry? If you are, write down what your priorities are, and what you want to achieve. Ask God and the Universe for what you want and be ready with open arms to accept your gift from God. Trust and let go. God only gives you the best because God loves you. The Universe is your best ally in time and space.

Money Practices

Now that you have learned to trust God, you can begin to understand the theory of the Law of Attraction in bringing what you want into your life. But this is only one side of the money story; the other side is the practical aspect of managing money. It will not serve you to attract the money you want into your life if you can't manage or respect money fully. Money may come into your life, but it can also very quickly leave if the conditions aren't right for it.

I am not going to give you a lesson on money management here, but I would like to share two practices I use that will provide you with the fundamentals of money management. Once you have made these practices part of your regular routine with money, you can learn about and use other techniques around money management and investment.

The first practice is to make sure you know exactly how much money you have in your bank account and in your wallet at all times, right down to the last penny. Sounds like hard work? It may be, but this is valuable information that will prevent you from over-spending or getting into debt. One of the lessons I learned was to respect money and not abuse it. I used to abuse money by over-spending. I used to spend without thinking about the consequences. I treated money like trash. I showed it no respect or care—no wonder I never had enough money to make ends meet. I never had a clue how much money I had in my account. I knew I got paid at the end of the month, but I never knew how much I was paid and I never knew exactly what was left after paying my essential bills, either. I always guessed what I had, but I was always wrong. I only discovered the real situation when my direct debit payments failed or when I couldn't get any money out of the cash machine. That was poor money management, and I was entirely to blame.

When I started to take care of my money, my entire financial situation changed. I am now able to attract money, keep it and make it grow. How do I do this? First of all, I keep a money journal. I record my income every time I'm paid, and I record the point when my outgoings are taken out of my account. I check the balance in my money journal against my online bank account every two weeks to make sure my own figures and those in my money journal tally.

By doing this, I have changed my spending habits. I am aware of how much money I have in my bank account, and so I know what I can or cannot spend. I know exactly how much money is going out of my account each day in direct debits and standing orders. I do not guess anymore; I know. This is a powerful practice that I recommend you follow, even if you do nothing else to manage your money.

"Many people take no care of their money till they come nearly to the end of it, and others do just the same with their time."
JOHANN WOLFGANG VON GOETHE

The second practice I use is the 10 per cent rule. I mentioned before that I always struggled to save money, and that I never had enough money to make ends meet, so I never had enough money to set aside for savings. After I changed the way I managed my money, my situation changed. After six months, I always knew exactly how much money I had in my bank account and in my wallet. That's when I decided to take up another challenge. I decided I would deduct 10 per cent of my income when it went into my bank account, and set that sum aside as savings. I had to make adjustments to my spending, of course, but the result has been well worth it.

When I started doing this, I was in debt and with all my outgoings, it felt very difficult at first. My conscious mind was freaking out, and I was feeling the pressure. When I first thought about setting aside 10 per cent of my income as savings, I couldn't breathe. This was my limiting belief showing up. I decided not to give in to my fears, and I put away my first 10 per cent and forgot about it. The following week, I did the same. It was a struggle because I was breaking a pattern I had formed over many years. It was hard, but my focus was on succeeding in putting myself in a better financial situation, so I was determined. I was done with my wasteful ways of living beyond my means.

After I'd made the fourth instalment, saving had become a new habit. More importantly, it was enjoyable and made me feel prosperous. I no longer felt stressed around money. I also developed new spending habits that supported my savings goal. I had a new money story and I knew things could only get better. Three years later, my savings have generated more income by earning interest. I have used the savings for holidays and gifts.

Please consider making this 10 per cent rule a habit for you as well. Wipe out your old patterns and beliefs about lack and not having enough. You can do it, and I can tell you that it's worth it. Once your subconscious mind has accepted this new pattern, it will be a joy to practise it. Give it a go and decide to see it through. I promise you won't regret it.

Lending and Borrowing

"Every time you borrow money, you are robbing your future self."

NATHAN W. MORRIS

Have you ever borrowed money from or lent money to friends and family? Have you lost money when lending money to friends and family? Have you ever borrowed money and never repaid it as you promised? This is a tricky subject, but I think it's important that we have a little discussion about this.

Yes, I am guilty of borrowing money from friends and family and failing to repay them. It feels terrible. When I am in this situation, I give away my power to them. I feel as if I owe them not just the money but everything else I have as well. If they ask a favour from me, I don't feel I can refuse because I owe them money. I am blessed to have loving and great friends, but I have borrowed money from them in the past and failed to repay them on time. They were cool about it because they are my friends and they understand and support me. They graciously accepted the revised repayment date and assured me that it was okay to slip up. It's okay to be imperfect and human.

Papa always says, "You can repay money, but you can never repay favours". Money is easy, you borrow it and you repay it. The kindness and favour shown to you when a family member or friend lends you money cannot be repaid, even if the money can. Remember, every thought and emotion has its own vibration and attracts events, people and circumstances that match the vibration, so manifesting your thoughts onto the silver screen of your life. When a family member or close friend asks you to do them a favour and lend them £200, what do you think and feel in that moment?

- Do you feel obliged to help?
- Do you feel worried that your friend will never repay you or pay you late so you can't keep your own financial commitments?
- What do you believe about lending money?

When you make a decision to lend money to someone, you make the decision based on your beliefs and your answers to the questions above. Whether you are lending the money from a place of financial comfort or with fear and doubt will determine the vibration you send out when the money changes hands, and the deal is sealed. If you have any negative beliefs or emotions around lending money, I urge you not to lend it. Only lend money to friends and family if you are prepared and able to lose the money. If you can't afford to lose the money, it would be much better to be honest and not lend it in the first place. Find a different way to help instead. If you cannot afford to lose the money, you will get annoyed, frustrated and even angry if your money is not returned to you when it is due. That will create a bad atmosphere between the two of you, and the other person is likely to feel uncomfortable knowing they have not been able to repay you as promised. You could end up losing a friend or a family member.

If you have positive beliefs and feelings about lending money, the money will be returned to you as promised. It might take longer to come back to you but it will return. Your energy around money is different when you let go of it. You can only do this when you have faith that the money will come back to you one way or another. Under these circumstances, you will feel comfortable helping your friend or family member you can relax and feel happy that you are able to help. That's because everything else—including getting the money back—has become secondary.

On another note; when you need money, before you ask your friends and family for help, ask yourself what your intention is around borrowing the money? Are you in debt and need immediate relief from creditors or bailiffs? Do you need the money for a new car? Do you need the money to fix your car? Do you need money to save your failing business?

What do you believe about borrowing money? Be very honest with yourself. Do you believe you can repay the money? What will be the consequences if you cannot repay it? How will you feel if you cannot repay it? Will you go into hiding and avoid the person who helped you because you are ashamed of yourself? Are you prepared to lose a friend or a family member because of a debt? Do you believe that your friend or family member will understand your situation and support you?

Think carefully before you answer. There is always another way to resolve any problem or issue than borrowing money. I am not telling you not to ask for help. I'm telling you to ask for help but ask for the right help. Ask with a full understanding of the consequences so you don't make promises you can't keep. Ask for help, having a full discussion with the person lending the money and make sure you both understand the consequences in order to prevent any misunderstandings or unrealistic expectations.

The Chinese always say, "When we talk about money there will be love lost one way or another." The Chinese believe in give and take. It is never our practise to go Dutch when we go out for a meal together or to ask someone to bring a contribution if they are invited to our home or to a party. The host always pays, and the guests pay the next time (should they wish, [words] an expectation). This next time might be years later; it doesn't matter. We never talk about money. This is the foundation of relationships in our culture. There is a clear, unwritten rule and understanding as to who will be paying for what on each occasion. We never fight over who is paying. We give without having any expectation of receiving. It is a mutually understood rule within our culture about who is paying for what.

- When they are earning, children, will always pay for their parents, grandparents or elderly relatives.

- Older brothers and sisters will always pay for younger sisters and brothers when the situation arises.
- Hosts always pay for guests.
- The person who is celebrating their birthday never has to pay for meals or take cakes to work for their colleagues. They are always spoilt by friends and family.
- Between friends, one friend pays one time and the other friend pays the next time.

So, only part with your money if you can do so with joy and without expectation. When you let your money go, do it joyously, and it will return to you a thousand times over. If you are unable to part with money joyously and without expectation, you would do better to say 'No' and look for a different way to help someone. In doing so, you can avoid damaging a relationship if your expectations of repayment are not met. Remember that there is always more than one way to resolve any problem in life. Money is an easy way but it's not the only way.

Getting Out of Debt

Are you in debt or have you ever been in debt? (If you have never experienced debt, be grateful because it is a difficult situation to be in.) How do we get into debt? Sometimes debt comes about due to circumstances and sometimes it is due to our relationship with money. If we have a poor relationship with money, debt is often the result. I have been in and out of debt many times in my life and when I look back, I realise it was often because of my own poor money management, poor judgement and limiting beliefs.

❋ *My Story*

In 2007, my business partner left the country taking £32,000 with him from the business account. He left me with the company's debts, including outstanding gas and electricity bills, tax bills, VAT bills, business rates and unpaid bills from suppliers. At the time, I was earning £1,600 a month from my day job as a surveyor. I could see no way to clear those debts with the income I had because after I had paid my own expenses, there was very little left over at the end of each month.

As a result, I was taken to court by the gas company and bailiffs came to our house. Our landline was constantly left off the hook, and I dared not open the mail. We lived in fear for the next three years. Every day, I woke feeling stressed and anxious, and I couldn't sleep at night. I was finally diagnosed with Type II Diabetes (I truly believed the Type II Diabetes came about due to the stress and my negative thought patterns, but I will say more about this in the section on Health and Wellbeing).

There was another time in my life when I couldn't make ends meet, too. My credit rating was really poor so getting credit was virtually impossible. My only option was to use payday and similar high-interest loans. These short-term loans took the pressure off me for a while as I would get a £200 loan to see me to the end of the month. I then paid off the loan and the interest when my salary was paid at the end of the month. I repeated this cycle month after month. Then Christmas came along. I had to find the money for gifts, social events, and food and drink. You know how it is. I bought gifts from a catalogue because I had some credit here, and everything went well over the festive period. Then January came. It is a long month, and I had very little money. That's when all hell broke loose!

I started to miss my payments. I couldn't afford to repay the catalogue in full, or the payday loan. One thing led to another, and I quickly accumulated a lot of debt. Both times when I got into debt, I did so because of my circumstances and my poor judgement. My emotional platform was one of lack, stress and worry so all I did was to attract more lack, stress and worry. It was a vicious circle.

Living in debt was one of the most stressful and horrible experiences I have ever been through. I felt as if I'd fallen into a bottomless pit and no matter how hard I tried, I couldn't get out. I couldn't think of anything but money and paying off my debts. I felt suffocated; all I wanted to do was sit in the dark, in silence and not be disturbed. In these dark, quiet moments, all I could think about was how stupid I had been and how angry I was with myself. I blamed everyone for failing to help me. I was full of regret, disappointment and fear.

But this was exactly what I needed to stop doing if I wanted to improve my situation. Why? Because what you focus on expands. The more I focused on my debts, the more debt I got into. The more

I focused on my fear, the more fear I experienced. The more I focused on my regrets, more things I regretted doing.

––––––––––––––––––––––

If you are in debt right now, I urge you to stop feeling and doing what I was feeling and doing and do this instead:

1) Do something you enjoy but haven't done for a while: watch a movie, listen to music, go for a walk, go fishing, go for a run, read a book, do some gardening, paint or engage in a craft like felting, sewing or knitting. I know it's difficult to focus on anything when you're in debt. I have been through the same experience; it is very challenging, but you need to get your mind off your problems and onto something else. You need to change your thinking and emotional platform.

2) Meditate in the evening and in the morning for five minutes each time to give your mind a break from worry.

3) Choose an affirmation that resonates with you and brings you a sense of peace. Repeat the affirmation throughout the day or when you notice that you start to worry.

4) Look at your situation from a practical point of view. How much do you owe? What is the worst that could happen if you can't pay? Is there any way you can negotiate a payment plan? Can you cope if the worst happens? Remember that it is only money. Yes, you have debts and your payments may be overdue, your creditors may send in the bailiffs or take you to court, but it's not a death sentence. As the Chinese say, "Where there is rainforest, you need not fear the lack of wood for fire." If your worst case scenario involves losing everything you own, it is okay. Material things come and go throughout our lives. As long as you are alive and kicking, you will be able to earn them back and very often, you'll get something better.

5) Change your beliefs about money and upgrade your money story. Learn the lessons from your situation and implement changes.

6) Take action. Take out a note book or sheet of paper or go to this link (www.havecourageliveyourpassion.co.uk) and list all your creditors in one column and the amount you owe to each

creditor in the second column. Create a plan, work out how much you can pay each of them. Alternatively, work at paying off the smallest amount first then move on to the next. Each time you make a payment, enter the new reduced amount you owe. Continue until you owe nothing to any of your creditors. Use this as a focus for visualisation: imagine seeing the sheet or page in your notebook showing zero against each creditor. (You will discover your net worth at the same time when you do this because the more debt you pay off, the higher your net worth will be.) Feel the relief and joy of being debt free. Feel proud that you have done it. Believing that it is achievable will help you through this experience.

Anchoring Your Prosperity

Money likes to be acknowledged and circulated. How often do you see something you want but deny yourself the joy of owning it or experiencing it, not because you cannot afford it, but because you have a limiting belief that says you can't have it? Next time, when you see something you really like, and you have the money for it, buy it. Give yourself a gift, love yourself. I am not encouraging you to go into debt or max out your credit card, but if you have the spare cash, buy it. Buy it with joy in your heart and with the belief that you are prosperous and that money will always circulate back to you. In doing so, you will be anchoring your success and making a statement to the Universe and your sub-conscious mind that you are wealthy. You are prosperous. You can have whatever you want in life. In taking this action, you are challenging and changing your limiting belief from 'lack' to 'plenty'.

❀ *My Story*

During my childhood, I learned not to expect new clothes or new toys. I didn't get new clothes until the old ones were worn out and had holes. Sometimes, I would be given 'hand-me-down' toys by neighbours or relatives. My auntie would give me and my brothers and sisters orange squash or biscuits that were past their sell-by date (her children were too precious to eat or drink them, but she thought we would be fine). In fact, my auntie actually believed we should have been grateful for out-of-date products because, but without her generosity, we would never have been able to afford them.

When I grew up, I rarely bought new clothes—I only got them if it was absolutely necessary. I never had smart clothes, only t-shirts and jeans. Clothes were not a priority for me. When I went window shopping, I would often see clothes I liked, handbags that got me excited, watches I hankered after and fabulously comfortable shoes, but I always convinced myself that I couldn't afford them or that I didn't need them. The truth was that it was my limiting beliefs, the blueprint that was firmly established in my subconscious mind, which was telling me that I do not deserve these nice new things. I did not believe I was worth it. These things were too good for me because they hadn't passed their sell-by date!

Money is energy and energy needs to be free-flowing. Money needs to circulate. I made my first statement of wealth when I bought a purse from Osprey in London for £110. It was a lot of money for me and a big step for someone who was not willing to pay more than £30 for any piece of clothing. That day, I made a statement to the Universe that I am anchoring myself at a new level of prosperity. I made a statement to my subconscious mind that I deserve to have what I want and I deserve to be prosperous.

———————————————

Anchoring your prosperity and success at a higher level doesn't need to be expensive. It's not about getting into debt or spending money you don't have. You could buy a CD you love, a meal at a restaurant you've always wanted to eat at or a night staying in your dream hotel. It is about changing your attitude or consciousness about money and what you deserve. It's about loving yourself, telling yourself you deserve to be happy and that you deserve to have the best you can afford. It's about enjoying the 'now' and being grateful for everything you have in your life at this moment in time. It's about having faith that money spent with joy will come back to you a thousand times over.

When money flows freely into your life, you will truly have the resources you want to pursue your aspirations, support your life mission and fuel your passion. Money is neutral; it is a tool that can help you live the life of your dreams.

CHAPTER EIGHT
Love and Relationships

"Some of the biggest challenges in relationships come from the fact that most people enter a relationship in order to get something; they're trying to find someone who's going to make them feel good. In reality, the only way a relationship will last is if you see your relationship as a place that you go to give, and not a place that you go to take."

ANTHONY ROBBINS

Romance is a beautiful thing in life. I love it. Do you have favourite singers, actors or actresses? Who is your celebrity crush? Who do you admire or are besotted with? Is it the actor or actress themselves or the characters they play? Theo James? Four? Ross Lynch? Chris Pine? Dove Cameron? Liv or Maddie? Zendaya? Zac Efron? Chris Hemsworth? Chris Evans? Captain America? Scarlett Johansson? Black Widow? Robert Downey Jr? Iron Man? I was told these people were 'untouchable' by ordinary people. We can only look at them and admire them. There is no way our paths or lives could ever cross, so we can only dream that we might be involved with them in some way. But is that true?

Let's look at it objectively. So far, we have learned that the Universe delivers whatever we focus on with energy and passion. But it's also true that the Universe can help us move towards our goals and dreams. It does this by giving us something that is better than we ever imagined or would have asked for. Let's look at this in more detail.

Tom is single and he is looking for a partner. He lives in Manchester. He sends out his request to the Universe. The Universe receives his message loud and clear and gets to work looking for the best match for Tom and calculating the quickest way to deliver Tom's future partner to him. However, it just so happens that Tom's ideal partner lives in Japan. The Universe will now re-arrange all the players and events in Tom's life and in his future partner's life to create a situation where they can meet. It could be a work conference in Japan or it could be a bizarre event that brings them together. But when they meet—bang! It will be love at first sight.

You never know how or when you will meet your ideal partner, soul mate, husband or wife. Your job is to send your request to God and trust God to deliver what you ask for. Be extremely honest with yourself and make a wish list the accurately describes the person you would like to share your life with. Never 'make do' or 'put up with', go for exactly what your heart desires; otherwise, you will have a lifetime of regrets, unfulfilled relationships and making do with what you get. It will be miserable for you, your partner and your children. What would your perfect partner look or be like? Get your journal out and start writing down your wish list. Below are some ideas to get you started:

1) As hot as Theo James.
2) A Nicole Kidman lookalike.
3) A similar age to me/two years older than me/younger than me.
4) Kind and understanding.
5) Blue eyes.
6) Brunette.
7) Treats me with respect at all times.
8) Caring and loving.
9) Does not smoke.
10) Does not gamble.
11) A gentleman/a lady.
12) Educated to Masters or PhD level.
13) Romantic and thoughtful.
14) Successful businessman or woman.
15) Excellent cook.
16) Loves travelling and reading.
17) Loves movies or archery or horse-riding.
18) Good sense of humour.
19) Generous.
20) Intelligent.

21) Wealthy and spiritual.

22) Loves geocaching.

23) Fun and a bit naughty.

24) Sporty and loves exercise.

25) Patient, kind or even-tempered.

What other traits or qualities would you like in your partner? What sort of person would you be compatible with? Who could be your soul mate? When considering what you want in your ideal partner, it's important you remember that no one can make you happy except YOU. If you want to find a partner or soulmate because you believe they will make you happy, the relationship will never work. You must be content and happy in yourself before setting out to attract your partner or soulmate. Happiness is an inside job.

- Don't fool yourself into thinking you will be able to put up with something about your partner just because you're in a relationship.
- Never enter into a marriage or long-term partnership believing you can change the other person.

Many women have this romantic idea that if our husband or partner loves us enough, they will do anything for us, including changing their habits or what they do. I'm not saying this is impossible, it only happens when the other person wants to change not because someone wants to change them. The decision to change comes from someone's own will and desire to change, not from their partner.

❋ *My Story*

When I got married, my husband, David, was a smoker. I wanted him to give up, but no matter how hard I tried to persuade him, he wouldn't do it. He smoked for the first nine years of our marriage despite knowing how much I disliked it. One day, Hannah came home from school and saw her daddy smoking. She burst into tears. (Hannah was only five years old, but she had already learned about the dangers of smoking at school.) She was very upset to see her daddy smoking. She asked her daddy to give up and within three months, David had completely given up smoking, and he has not touched a cigarette since.

Hannah tugged at his heartstrings when she cried over his smoking and begged her daddy to give up. David loves Hannah too much to consciously do anything to upset her. It was Hannah's reaction that made David take a firm decision to change. But he changed because he wanted to change. It was a decision based on the love of a father for his daughter.

The only person we can change is ourselves. We cannot force anyone to do anything they do not want to do. This is law. God is a God of freewill. God does not force his will on you or me, so he will not impose your will on others for any reasons.

Let's look at another story.

Let's say you met a handsome guy. Let's call him Theo. He is a handsome, intelligent, funny and kind guy, and he seems to be everything you want in a man. But after a few dates, you find out that he has some little habits that make you uneasy or that you find annoying. For example, he has to lick his index finger so he can turn the page of a book or newspaper. You discover that he sticks his fingers inside the glass when he carries it from the dishwasher to the cupboard. You find out that he often goes to casinos. For arguments sake, let's say these are your pet hates. You look at Theo and because you love him, you think you can put up with these annoying habits. After all, they are only habits; they're not life or death issues. You decide these irritations won't spoil your relationship. You decide that when he finds out that these habits annoy you, he will be willing to change them so he can prove how much he loves you. Of course you are not going to spell it out for him. You will ask him to change his ways but keep back the bit about it, being a way for him to prove his love for you. You will start judging his love for you from his 'Performance' or progress in changing those annoying habits you hate so much.

Men cannot read minds. Women can't read minds either. Theo only thinks that he has been asked to change his habits because you don't like them. He doesn't know that it is his way to prove his love to you. Theo does not see changing those habits as crucial to making the relationship work, so he sees no reason to change. He doesn't really want to change, but he says he'll try. But because he doesn't really want to change, his efforts are half-hearted. You are watching him like a hawk to see signs that he is changing. You silently and secretly grade his effort by giving marks out of 10 every day. You see no change, so you start to doubt his love for you. Despite your requests, he still licks his fingers before turning a page, he still sticks his fingers in the glasses and he still goes to the casino on a Friday night with his friends.

How do you feel now? You start to second guess Theo's true feeling for you. You come up with stories to make sense of it all, to prove your theory correct. You have created a story that says Theo does not love you as much as you believe he should because he still goes to the casino. He clearly loves his friends more than you. If he loved you, he would have stopped licking his finger before turning a page, and he would carry those glasses the way you asked him to. Can you see how this story you are telling is just getting you into a deeper and deeper hole while Theo is oblivious to the game you are playing? You start to find fault with him more and more; the relationship can never work in such hostile conditions.

Here are some other examples of this kind of rule:

- If he gave up smoking, it would prove he loves me.
- If he stops gambling, it means he truly loves me.
- If he gives up golf, it shows he loves me so I will stay with him.

This way of testing whether our partner loves us is a silly game. It is our insecurity and need for assurance that drives us to set these tests. Relationships are based on love, trust, respect and an understanding of each other's values and beliefs. Both sides need to be open with each other. It is like baking a cake. Every cake has a recipe that we must follow in order to make a successful cake. The basic ingredients for most cakes are the same—flour, butter, eggs and sugar. However, for chocolate cake, we add oil and chocolate powder; for fruit cake, we add mixed fruits; for Victoria Sponge, we add buttercream and jam, so on and so forth. Each relationship has its own recipe that makes it special, but the basic ingredients are the same.

Write your wish list for your ideal partner and send your request to God and the Universe for the perfect person to come into your life, be cool. Don't get discouraged if they don't show up immediately. If the person you are with right now does not tick every single box on your list, let it go. If he/she is the right person, things will work out. If he/she is not the right person, forcing the relationship by 'putting up with them' or trying to change them will not result in a happy ending. Have faith and be patient.

The right person is just around the corner and will come into your life, probably when you least expect it. Be open-minded.

Enjoy the company of your friends and the time with your colleagues. Relax, chill out and enjoy life. Don't get too hung up on the details. You have all the time in the world. When you are ready, the perfect person for you will come along. Concentrate on being happy now.

✳ *Ana and Alan's Story*

Ana was a devout Catholic who had been married to Alan for over 40 years. They had one son. When I met Ana, she had bruises on her face and arms. She said she'd fallen, but the evidence said otherwise.

Ana is a caring, warm and kind lady. She helped me find my way back to my room when I first arrived in Portsmouth. It was the second day of my adventure in the UK, and I had gone out for a walk, but I couldn't find my way back. Ana spoke to me, took me to her home, dug out the local map and showed me how to get back to the place where I was renting a room for the summer. We became friends. Ana took me under her wing, checking on me to make sure I was eating properly and coping with a new culture.

One day, Ana phoned me from the hospital. I didn't know how she had got her injuries, but it didn't look as if she had fallen off her bicycle as she told me she had. Later, she told me that Alan beat her whenever he'd had too much to drink. This had been going on for over 30 years. Ana had been putting up with the violence for a long time. My heart sank when I heard her story. How could such a lovely woman with a heart of gold be treated like this by a man who was supposed to love her and had made a vow to take care of her?

Alan passed away in 2005. He lost his life to cancer. A couple of years later Ana met Stephen. She seemed happy for a while but soon she came to me with injuries that were very much like the ones I had seen before. Stephen started to hit her when he'd had too much to drink. Ana was stuck in a cycle, trapped by her own limiting beliefs, negative thoughts patterns and low expectations.

We all make poor decisions at times; we are all human after all. This is the way we learn. If you have made a poor decision in your relationship, have the courage to put things right. Don't settle for what you have if it isn't right.

Take a closer look at your relationship and see if you can spot the limiting beliefs and thought patterns that have created the situation you are in. See if you can understand what limiting beliefs have governed your partner's thought patterns and behaviours. Once you understand the limiting beliefs you both hold, you may be able to work things out and resolve any conflict or misunderstandings between the two of you. It is important to remember that at some time in the past, something magical did happen between the two of you. Otherwise you would not be where you are today. So, what has changed? What went wrong? When did it start to go wrong? Do you know why? Can you forgive your partner or yourself for whatever that has happened? Can you forgive each other? Are you willing to work on the limiting beliefs and thought patterns that have created these experiences?

When you truly love someone, you can forgive anything. However, most of the time, it is our ego that stops us from doing what is right. Our heart wants to forgive, but our head tells us that if we forgive there will be no justice, or if we forgive them, the other person will think it is fine to continue with their bad behaviour. This may be true, but forgiveness is for us rather than for those who have done us wrong. Forgiveness is for our peace and for releasing the blocks that are preventing us from receiving the good things in life. Forgiveness fills our hearts with love, peace and serenity. When you are at peace, you will be open to inspiration from God and the Universe and you will be open to new ideas, hunches or instincts that will guide you in solving your problems.

If you are not willing to forgive, you will be bitter and possibly consumed with anger, hurt, disappointment, frustration, and other destructive emotions. You will not be thinking straight so you will be too uptight to hear or become aware of new ideas and inspiration from God. The Universe may be knocking at your door, but you will not be answering because all you can hear is the voice of your partner arguing with you or your own thoughts running over the same incident over and over again. Whether you decide to stay in a relationship or leave your partner, start with forgiveness. Once you forgive, everything else will fall into place.

Respect and Understanding

When you are in a relationship, the first thing you need to do is respect your partner so you can understand the person you are with. What makes them tick? What is important to them? What are their pet hates? When is it best to stay away and when best to offer comfort? Respect them and respect their quirks even though it may not seem reasonable or make sense to you. Think about the following story.

It was Sunday afternoon, and I was enjoying it by watching an episode of Pretty Little Liars on television. Dinner was going to be boiled bacon with peas pudding, buttered cabbage and new potatoes. I had also planned to cook a batch of Bolognese sauce and freeze it so we would have a quick meal available during the week. My plan was to start cooking both dishes after the television programme finished at around 5pm. At 4:30pm, my husband came into the living room and saw me watching the television. I told him I will start cooking when the programme is finished. The next thing I knew; he was in the kitchen chopping the vegetables for the Bolognese. Why was he doing that? What would be your reaction if you were in my shoes? My reaction was driven by my belief system.

I became angry because he had started preparing the vegetables despite the fact that I had told him that I would be doing it after the programme finished at 5pm. I felt that he was interfering with my plans, and I did not appreciate it. I felt he was implying that I was not doing what I was supposed to be doing—cooking dinner and Bolognese—but sitting and watching TV.

These were the thoughts that were going through my head, whether they were true or not didn't matter. My limiting beliefs concluded that my husband was not trying to help but was interfering and implying that I was not doing my 'job' properly. Either that or he thought I wasn't capable of cooking two dishes at the same time.

In fact, my husband's intention was a noble one. He cares about me and so he wanted to help. He thought he would prepare the vegetables so they were ready when I started cooking at 5pm. He was not trying to make a point or imply anything by his actions. His criticism of me was all in my head. It was my own interpretation that caused the misunderstanding.

The truth is that I like to do everything. I love cooking, and it is important to me that I do everything from start to finish when I make a dish. I don't like anyone around me trying to help or asking for instructions. So my husband's good intentions simply stressed me out and took away my precious time in the kitchen. If my husband understood this part of me, he could respect my wishes and not interfere by doing things for me. On the other hand, if I understood and respected my husband's wish to help me and his desire to show he cares about me, I would not have reacted the way I did. I simply would have felt love instead of anger and irritation.

How many times have you and your partner gone through similar episodes? When has one person done something out of love only to find that their kindness has been perceived by the other person as wrong or unwanted? These actions created unnecessary conflicts and in the long run, affected your relationship?

From now on, when something like this happens, take a deep breath and a take a step back. Look at the event dispassionately until you become aware of the intention of both parties before you make a judgement. In fact, ask yourself whether you need to react at all? Is this something worth damaging your relationship for? Perhaps, instead of 'reacting', you could choose to have a chat about it like two sensible adults? Whatever you do, please do not choose to walk away from dealing with it. If you do not deal with it at the time, it will happen again. Every incident in life is there to teach us a lesson or show us something we needed to know. Otherwise, similar events will keep showing up until you and your partner learn from the situation and resolve the issue.

Relationships and business are very similar. It is relatively easy to start a business but it takes time, nurture, passion, love, planning, understanding, communication, skill and respect to be successful in business. It's the same with relationships. Successful relationship requires time, love, passion, respect, nurture, planning, communication, thought, understanding and much more to succeed. It will be much easier if your partner is compatible with you, and it will be more fun if your partner is your soulmate. When you find the right person to share your life with, the lows will be more bearable and the highs will be more meaningful. So, trust God and the Universe to bring you the perfect person to share your life with. Write your wish list today then be open to meeting the love of your life today.

CHAPTER NINE
Health and Wellbeing

STOP! STOP THINKING about illness! Look around you. How many people do you know or meet or even live with who are ill in some way? As a surveyor, I usually go to many different properties every day so I see a lot of sick people. Their ailments range from headaches, migraines, depression, general discomfort and work-related stress all the way through to MS and cancer. When I listen to their conversations, their language and the stories they relate and show it is no coincidence that they are in such poor health because your beliefs and thoughts create your emotions and these affect your life. So that means your beliefs create your experiences.

❀ *My Story*

During the darkest years of my life from 2007-2011, my world crumbled around me because my emotional platform was fear, anger, frustration, lack, sadness, betrayal, hopelessness and loss. It all started when my business partner left with all the money from the business leaving me to deal with the aftermath of debt and failure.

We started a business in 2005 and I re-mortgaged my family house in order to raise capital to get it started. My business partner left in 2007 with £32,000 of my money. The business was a Chinese Restaurant in Portsmouth. My business partner ran the day to day business, and I was an investor. I kept doing my day job because I didn't know much about running a restaurant. I helped start the business because I wanted to help my business partner start a career. I trusted him. I loved him. He was my younger brother, the 'Golden Pomelo' in my late grandma's eyes.

After my brother left, I discovered that he had not been paying the bills, the taxes or any of his suppliers for at least six months. He had cancelled all the direct debits I had set up to ensure the bills and taxes would be paid automatically. It was my own fault. I should have checked. That's a lesson I have learned the hard way. But the pain of being betrayed by my own brother, that's another story...

I was hurt. I was lost. I lived in fear for two and a half years. I jumped when the doorbell rang, and I wished every day was a Sunday so that there wouldn't be any post. I disconnected my landline so the phone wouldn't ring, and my mobile was on silent all the time. I didn't answer any calls if I didn't recognise the number. I didn't sleep at night for worrying about the debts and what had happened. I was consumed by anger and hatred for my brother, and what he had done to me.

In 2009, I was diagnosed with Type II Diabetes. I believe this was a result of the constant stress and destructive emotions I had experienced for over two years. Although I wasn't specifically thinking about diabetes or about getting ill, I was emotionally drawn to it. My emotional platform was destructive. When I felt the anger, sadness, hatred, betrayal and fear and didn't get any proper rest or sleep. I was battering my body so I became ill with the toxic imbalance of chemicals. If I had not got Type II Diabetes, I would have become ill with something else.

While doing research for this book, I came across an article Dr Thomas Willis, a 17th century English doctor who specialised in anatomy, neurology and psychiatry. Dr Willis speculated that diabetes was caused by "long sorrow and other depression". In fact, he identified the significance of sugar in the development of diabetes mellitus. His observations show how much impact our thoughts and emotions play in our health and wellbeing.

Fortunately, I believed I could reverse my diagnosis as I believed my diabetes was a temporary blip. I knew that Type II Diabetes can be successfully reversed because I had read books such as Blood Sugar Diet by Dr Michael Mosley. I also knew that The Gerson Institute, a non-profit organisation in San Diego, California was dedicated to providing education and training in Gerson Therapy, an alternative and non-toxic treatment for cancer and other chronic degenerative diseases including diabetes, heart disease, auto-immune disorders, arthritis and many others.

Placebo Effects

A placebo is a fake medication or treatment given to patients, with or without the patient's knowledge. Placebos can include anything from a pill without any active ingredient, a saline injection or a sham surgery. The whole point of using a placebo is to test whether a medication is having an impact due to its active ingredient or because the patient believes it works.

Over the years, doctors and scientists have conducted many trials and studies to monitor the effective of placebos on patients. During these trials, one group of patients will be given the actual drug or surgery and another group will be given the placebo. The results are interesting. The percentage of a placebo group experiencing results from their treatment is similar to those receiving real treatments. So why do placebos work?

❋ *Grandma's Story*

My late grandma lived in a village so the nearest doctor was in the local town, Tanjung Tualang. One day, when I got home from college and my grandma told me she'd had stomach ache since the morning. It was late afternoon by then, and she was still in pain. We didn't have a car at the time, and there were no taxis in the village so we had no way of getting her to the doctor. Grandma was in so much pain she could hardly stand up so Mama went to our neighbour and asked for help. The neighbour had a car and was able to take Grandma to the doctor in town.

As soon as we reached the clinic, grandma seemed calmer and her pain lessened. We registered grandma with the doctor and sat down to wait for our turn to be seen. We only waited about 10 minutes to be called, but by that time Grandma was able to walk into the consultation room as if nothing had happened—all her pain had subsided. How was this possible? Mama said grandma had been so ill all day she hadn't eaten anything. But her symptoms eased as soon as we reached the clinic and had completely gone by the time she was called in to see the doctor.

What had helped my grandma get better so fast was her belief in doctors. She particularly trusted her own doctor who we went to see in Tanjung Tualang. Grandma believed that doctors had the power to make her well. This was because whenever she was ill or poorly, she felt better as soon as she saw her doctor. So as soon as Grandma got to the doctor's surgery her subconscious mind convinced her that she was going to get well, so she did. The doctor acted as a placebo, so even though he didn't do anything, my grandma's belief in his powers to make her better meant she got better almost instantly.

The Power of Conditioning

When my brothers and sisters and I were little, whenever we were poorly or we hurt ourselves, we were rushed to the hospital or the local doctor's surgery. There, we were met by adults in white coats, all assuring us we would be better very soon. Our parents look relieved and had a big smile on their faces when the man or woman in the white coat delivered the message that all was well.

From this experience, we became conditioned to believe that a doctor is the person who makes us better when we are injured or ill. How many of us automatically suggest to our friends and family that they 'see a doctor' whenever they describe having any pain or physical discomfort? I know I'm guilty of dishing out this kind of advice. That's because we trust the man or woman in the white coat with a stethoscope dangling around their necks. Whatever they say or prescribe we believe will heal us or make us better.

We give our entire health and wellbeing over to doctors. When a doctor delivers bad news to a patient, he or she is as good as signing their death certificate at that very moment. This is because most of us have been conditioned to believe that doctors know everything about our bodies and health. So if they say we have three months left to live, we believe it is true and unquestionable. In the same way, if a doctor assures us that we will heal without even a scar, this is what happens. We accept that as true with questioning it. A placebo works because we are conditioned to believe that doctors are healers and so whatever they give us will make us better. It's all in our mind.

The Power of the Subconscious Mind

Our subconscious mind is an amazing part of our psychological makeup. It is the most powerful mental tool that we have. It operates every single organ and cell in our body, both during the day and night. We don't consciously know how to make our heart beat or our lungs breathe, but we don't need to because our subconscious mind does it for us.

When we believe we will be helped or healed by a specific drug or surgery, our subconscious mind gets to work and releases the necessary endorphins and neurotransmitters that activate the parasympathetic nervous system. It increases our immunity and does whatever it takes to generate self-healing in line with the unconscious instruction to get better. The placebo is the message from our conscious mind to our subconscious mind to make us well.

I am not medically trained as a nurse or doctor so if you're interested in finding out more about how we can heal ourselves with our brain, I recommend that you read Mind Over Medicine by Dr Lissa Rankin and You Are The Placebo by Dr Joe Dispenza. These books will help you understand how our beliefs and psyches affect our health and wellbeing.

The Nocebo Effect

A nocebo is similar to a placebo, except that it has the capacity to make us ill rather than better. There are not many trials or experiments carried out exploring the nocebo effect as it is considered unethical for doctors to put patients through trials that have the potential to damage their life.

Like a placebo, the impact of a nocebo is on the mind rather than the body. If you believe that the drugs or surgery prescribed will not help or will make you worse then that's what will happen. In the same way, a nocebo can work simply in the form of bad news about health. When someone is told something is wrong with him, he begins to have the symptoms even if the diagnosis is wrong or mistaken—or just a downright lie. This explains why some patients are healed by treatment and others are not. Even though the same drugs or treatments might be prescribed to two people, it's the person who believes the treatment will work who will get well. The person who is uncertain, disbelieving or sceptical is unlikely to get better simply through the intervention of a doctor. This proves that doctors are only part of the healing process and that patients have a huge impact on their health and well-being, too.

Multiple Personality Disorder

What multiple personality disorder has got to do with health and well-being, you may ask. Well, I am interested in how a patient's switch from one personality to another also changes their physiology. It shows how the mind can affect the body in extraordinary way. Patients with multiple personality disorder experience a powerful psychological separation between one personality and another. Each of the personalities has his or her own name, age, abilities, illness, allergies, memories, style of writing, cultural background, talents, languages and even eye colour!

Dr Bennett Braun of the International Society for the Study of Multiple Personality Disorder in Chicago documented a case where all of a patient's different personalities became allergic to orange juice, except one. If the personality with the allergy drank the orange juice, rashes would break out. However, if he switched to his non-allergic personality, the rash would instantly start to fade and he could drink the orange juice without experiencing any medical issues.

In one case, a patient with multiple personality disorder was admitted to the hospital with complications resulting from diabetes. Her doctors were baffled when she switched personality and was suddenly displayed no symptoms of the condition. These studies prove how powerful our brain is and that it is capable of changing us physically. There is also evidence that we can heal ourselves when we have a strong enough belief in the power of the subconscious mind.

When it comes to our health, it is clear that doctors and medicine only play a small part in curing us. The rest of the healing process is down to us. That's why it's important that children are taught that while doctors dress the wound, it is God that heals. Doctors do not actually heal, they do what they can to help the actual healing, but we only get well through God and the power of our subconscious minds.

If you are in good health at the moment, give thanks and be grateful. Think healthy thoughts and never worry that you will be affected by disease or illness, not even hereditary ones. If you are unwell at the moment, choose to believe that you can heal. Be grateful for what you have at this moment in time. Use affirmations, meditation and visualisations to promote healing. Have faith and never give up no matter what anyone says to you.

The Power of Suggestion

In Chinese culture, we believe in mediums, fortune tellers, ghosts, reincarnations and everything that is magical and mysterious. The nearest city to my village when I was growing up was Ipoh and in that village there was a famous medium who everyone knew as Sister Ying. She was so sought-after that she started seeing people at 5am and finished around lunch time. People believe that the best time for a reading is in the early hours of the morning as it is the most auspicious time and when the readings are most accurate. Sister Ying was always booked well in advance no matter what time of year it was but getting an appointment with her in the lead-up to the Chinese New Year and Ching Ming (The season where all Chinese families visit their ancestors' graves) was especially difficult. You had to book at least six months in advance to see Sister Ying at this auspicious time.

Uncle Bill lived two streets away from our house. He wasn't my real uncle, but as children we were expected to address anyone older than us as sister, brother, uncle, auntie, gong-gong or poh-poh, depending on their age.

This particular year, Uncle Bill went for a Chinese New Year reading with Sister Ying. He had booked the appointment a year before, and he was hoping to hear a positive prediction for the year ahead, even something along the lines that he would be prosperous in the approaching Year of the Dragon. He hoped to hear he would have lots of luck with the lottery and that his business would be extremely successful. Well, that was what he hoped for, but the actual prediction was nothing like that, not even close.

Sister Ying dished out a prediction of death by Ching Ming, which was just six weeks later. Nothing could have prepared Uncle Bill for this. He was in his fifties, and he was healthy. Sister Ying predicted a heart attack; Uncle Bill was very unhappy to say the least. He was in shock and could not believe that he was going to die in six weeks.

Uncle Bill started to make preparations for his death despite his family and friends trying to tell him that it was just a reading and not accurate. They told him he should not read too much into it. His wife convinced him to get a medical check at the hospital. The result was very good, his cholesterol level was fine, his blood pressure was good and his blood sugar was normal. There were no signs of any illness. Over the following weeks, Uncle Bill concentrated on doing his paperwork and getting his affairs in order. He saw to his accounts, sorted out his assets, and he met with solicitor so he could make sure his wife and children would be taken care of after he was gone. Uncle Bill totally believed the prediction because of Sister Ying's credentials. She was famous and apparently never got a single prediction wrong.

As Ching Ming approached, Uncle Bill started to complain about aches and pains that he'd never had before. He started to feel faint at times and became lethargic. On the actual day of Ching Ming, everyone was busy preparing to visit their ancestors' graves. Uncle Bill told his family that he was very tired and didn't wish to go. His family went without him. Uncle Bill lay down for an afternoon nap and never woke up. The cause of death given was 'heart attack'. How does a healthy man fade away within weeks just because of a prediction by a medium? This is the power of the subconscious mind. In this case, Sister Ying was the nocebo. Uncle Bill believed her completely, and his subconscious mind delivered his death as she predicted.

You Control Your Health

The power to control your health is within you. It is your birth-right to have good health, prosperity and success. It is your choice whether you have good health and a wonderful life. Do not give away your power and your birth-right to someone else. You may be ill or in the last stages of your precious life on earth but you can always aid your healing by choosing to live.

So whatever you do, never give up. Never give in to the challenges of ill health. I appreciate that you may be feeling exhausted, and you may have lost all hope but look around, open your heart and mind and you will see miracles everywhere. It is up to you to accept these miracles or let them pass you by. People who have accepted these miracles are telling their stories to give strength and hope to others in a similar situation. People who have been told they just have three months left to live have been completely healed of cancer and gone on to live to a ripe old age. They have different genetics and different illnesses as they come from different races, sexes and countries, but they have one thing in common they never gave up, they never gave in. They believed there was another way and they found it. If there is only one thing you will take away from this book, take this:

'Choose life and never give up.'

CHAPTER TEN
Manifestation Tools

BEFORE I GO, I would like to leave you with a few simple tools that will help you to create a meaningful and fulfilling life. These tools will help you to centre yourself and manifest your thoughts. You don't have to use every single tool, just choose the ones you like and enjoy and start using them.

"Do the difficult things while they are easy, and do the great things while they are small. A journey of a thousand miles must begin with a single step."

LAO TZE

Affirmations, Meditations and Creative Visualisations

Affirmations are a good tool to use when you want to change your limiting beliefs. When you start using them, the affirmations may sound like a lie to you, but keep using them because eventually, your subconscious mind will accept them as true and that is when your life will begin to change. How fast that happens depends on the strength of your limiting belief and how willing you are to let them go. I have used affirmations that have worked within 24 hours, but I also used affirmations that took much longer to have an impact, especially If what I wanted to change was important to me. Effective affirmations have three important elements if they are going to work: they need to be relevant, positive and present.

Relevant

Relevant means the affirmation must be relevant to you and your situation. You need to know what you want in the area of life you want to change or improve. Is it money, career, relationship, health or all of them? Take out your journal and write one title on each page so that you have a dedicated page for each area of life you wanted to work on. Take 5 to 10 minutes to write down what you would like in each area. It has to be something you really want, not what you think you want or what you think your parents would like you to have or your boyfriend or girlfriend or partner want you to have. Listen to you heart and write it down, no matter how ridiculous or impractical it might sound to you. This is your journal, and you don't have to show it to anyone else. So, go ahead, be honest and start writing. Have fun.

Positive

Positive means using positive statements or words. Write down what you want, not what you do not want. Use phrases such as: 'I can afford', 'I can have', 'I have the skills', 'I have the ability'. Never use phrases like: 'I try' or 'I will try' or 'I can't afford' or 'I don't have'.

Present

Write your affirmations as if what you want has already happened or your affirmation has been manifested. If you use the phrase 'I will find a job' or 'I will own my dream car', that is where your car and job will stay—in the future. It will never arrive. Say your affirmation as if it is now and as if it has happened today. Affirm what you want with emotion. Imagine the emotions you will feel when your request has been delivered by the Universe i.e. happy, excited, ecstatic or something else. Feel that feeling when you say your affirmations. You need to convince your subconscious mind that you mean business, so don't be wishy-washy with your instructions. If you are a team leader or a manager, you know you need to give firm instructions to your team members so they understand that you are willing to act on your instructions. It is the same with your subconscious mind: be firm and be clear. Here are some examples of affirmations you can use or adapt for your own purposes:

- I am a straight-A student, and I am doing extremely well in all my studies.
- I am a successful author and international speaker.

- I am earning £___ a year, doing a job I love, while also having more fun and family time than ever before.
- I am working from home, earning £___ a month, doing a job I love.
- I am a money magnet, and unexpected income is always coming to me.
- I am joyfully and gratefully receiving £___ in unexpected income today.
- I am creative and resourceful in fulfilling all my financial needs.
- I am grateful that all my needs are met by the Universe, and God is the source of my supply.
- I am an excellent money manager.
- I am one of the best surveyors in the company.
- I am one of the best in the organisation.
- My income is constantly increasing, and I have £___ in my savings account on 31 December 20xx.
- All the money I need for taxes, school fees and expenses are provided for me. I am grateful for the abundance of the Universe.
- I am so photogenic that I cannot have a bad photo.
- I have an attractive body that is the perfect weight. I am slim and beautiful.
- I enjoy excellent health.
- I am healed. Thank you, thank you and thank you!
- My body is strong and healthy.
- I approve and accept myself.
- I love and accept myself, just as I am.
- I am willing to accept love. I deserve love.
- I am grateful for my soul mate, and the wonderful times we are sharing.

Use affirmations with faith. Do not doubt the instructions that you give to your subconscious mind. For example, if you say your affirmations every morning for five minutes with emotion and passion while you feel happy, avoid undermining the effect with negative thoughts later in the day. Thinking negative thoughts will confuse the Universe as to whether you really want what you said so it doesn't know whether to fulfil your earlier instructions or not.

So, say your affirmations with feeling and make sure you mean it. Throughout the day, when you notice that your worries and doubts are coming up, stop immediately and say your affirmations. Drown out that little voice that is trying to bring you back down with declarations. A declaration is an affirmation with teeth. Sing your affirmation or write it down lots of times on a piece of paper. Engage your mind in doing something so you do not give in to the little devil of negativity. Tell your negative thoughts that you are the boss and that you are not messing about.

When you write down your affirmations, they will have twice as much impact. If you say your affirmations during a meditation and introduce a visualisation to your mind at the same time, it will make them even more potent. Here's how I meditate every night before I go to sleep.

Meditation

Lie in bed and get comfortable. Relax by closing your eyes and breathing in through your nose and out slowly through your mouth. Clear your mind. Continue the breathing sequence until you feel calm and peaceful.

At this point, start thinking about your affirmations. Say them quietly to yourself several times. When you feel comfortable, visualise what it will be like when your affirmations become reality. How will you feel and what will you do? Create the picture in your mind and create a mind movie of yourself enjoying it.

If your affirmation is about your career, work out what needs to happen for you to know that your affirmation has been manifested? Is it an award or having your own office? Maybe you can imagine your boss delivering the news to you. Create that movie in your mind, hear what is said, feel what you will feel and enjoy your mind movie.

If it is money you want, what is it that you want to happen? Do you want to win the lottery? Do you want a pay cheque of £50,000? Do you want 300 internet orders coming through to your online shop every day? Do you want a particular sum of money in the bank? Or do you want to see yourself sweeping up £50 notes in your front gardens and filling up five sacks with it? Be as creative and as ridiculous as you want. It is your mind movie. It is there to make you happy and lift your level of vibration so you are open to the abundance of the Universe.

What about your health? Imagine the doctor delivering the 'all clear' news to you? See yourself throwing your medication in the bin because you no longer need it? See yourself being happy and running, maybe leaving your wheelchair behind? Again, be creative.

If you can do the meditation twice a day while incorporating your affirmations and visualisation at the same time, your affirmations will become even more effective and powerful and your desires will manifest much faster in your life.

Journal

Writing is a powerful tool for manifesting your goals and dreams. When you write, you engage your brain by focusing your attention on what you want, thereby creating positive emotions. First, go and buy a journal that you love then start writing.

While writing in your journal, concentrate on your wishes, dreams, aspirations and goals. You can write bullet points or full paragraphs. You could also write a letter to the Universe or God telling them how you feel or what you would like to have happen in your life. You could also write to a close friend (Without sending it), telling your friend about your achievements. If you are going to an interview you feel nervous about, it's a good idea to fast forward to the point where you are offered the job then write a letter to your best friend or your parents telling them how you went through the interview, and how excited you are to be offered the job. Here's something I wrote in my journal on 5 October 2012:

1) I am financially stable, with a job that brings in at least £4,000 every month.

2) I want to shop at Waitrose every week.

When I wrote those two requests, I had been unemployed for 18 months. My first request was delivered to me in May 2014. Writing my wishes or requests gave me hope so I had something to look forward to. The second wish was granted in 2015. It did not start to work until I crossed out the words 'want to shop' with my red pen and replaced it with 'am shopping' in the sentence. It changed my emotions and my thoughts every time I read the sentence. This shows how important it is to write in the present tense when creating affirmations, goals, aspirations or wishes. On 10 February 2013, I wrote the following passage to calm my nerves as I had an interview coming up. It was the first job interview I had for nearly two years:

"Wow! It was a great interview. I enjoyed it. My interviewers were really impressed with my approach and answers to their questions. We had a great rapport. I am happy, excited and looking forward to my new job. I know I have done the best I can in the interview, I am happy, satisfied, contented and grateful for the opportunity. Thank you, thank you and thank you."

After writing this in my journal, I read it over many times, especially whenever I started to feel nervous about the interview. It changed my emotional state. When you read, you can't help but create a story in your mind or what I called a visualisation. This statement made me happy, and I felt prepared for the actual event. The event happened exactly as I had written about it. It was amazing. On 18 February 2013, I was offered the job after a successful interview.

When I decided to leave that job, I said to myself that it would be great if I could get a job where I could work from home earning at least double my current salary. My take home pay was £1,600 a month. The new job I was offered was exactly what I had requested. I won the role of team leader of the surveying team. I worked from home and my take-home pay was more than double my pay at my previous job. I was there for 13 months.

I have had many other goals, aspirations, heart-felt desires manifested in ways that I could never have imagined. Things just happened without much effort from me. My job was to ask and show up by taking action. When I took one step, God and the Universe took 10 steps for me. God and the Universe always know the best and fastest way to deliver my requests to me.

Next, take out your journal and start writing your own requests. Read them over three to four times each day to keep yourself focused on what you want then trust God and the Universe to deliver what you want to you. All you need to do is to show up and take action towards making your dreams a reality. Be ready for fantastic results.

Vision Boards and Vision Books

This is a tool I use to help me visualise what I want. I have two vision boards in my study, both filled with pictures of beautiful homes and holiday locations. There are objects such as coffee makers, I'd like to have, cars I want to own and rooms whose interior designs I love. I also have images of the first class cabins of major airlines and pictures of conference halls filled with audiences (to depict my success as an international speaker). When I look at the board every day, it makes me happy, and I visualise my success effortlessly.

If you don't have space for a vision board, you can use a vision book instead. I have a vision book where I keep images of all the holiday destinations I'd like to visit, pictures of my dream home, images of happy successful people, a million-pound bank note, my bank statement with my desired bank balance on it, the fire place I want in my dream home, and so on.

I change the pictures from time to time as I receive items on the board and my desires are fulfilled. I replace them with something new such as the picture of a car I would like. I have a picture of a Ford Kuga and Hyundai ix35. It's not the make or model I focus on but the type of car I like. I won't grumble if I have a Citron C5 or Kia Shortage instead of what is on the board or in the vision book. I added the picture of a Hyundai ix35 in 2014 and in July 2015, I was a proud owner of that exact car.

If you can't find a picture of what you want, you can write a description of it on a piece of paper or card and pin it up on your board or into your book. For example, if you are in financial difficulty and would like to improve your credit rating, write your ideal credit score on a piece of paper as a way of affirming your desired credit score. I have written a note stating that I have money to pay the school fees on time and in full each term. I put that note in my vision book and read it every day. Start a vision board or a vision book or both today. Refer to it every day. Have fun. It will help to raise your vibration, keep you focused on what you want and help you to visualise receiving it.

Practise Gratitude

I would say that expressing gratitude is the most important and fundamental tool in manifesting your dream life. When you are grateful and happy right now, The Universe will deliver more of what you want that matches your vibrations and emotions. How do you express gratitude? Below are examples of what you must never say.

- When I lose the weight, I will be happy.
- When I get my degree, I will be happy.
- I would be a thrill if I was shortlisted in the writing competition.
- I will be happy if I can reach my sales target this month.
- I will be happy if my dad buys me that car.
- I will grateful if I am healed.
- I will be grateful if I can earn £100,000 a year.

These statements are what people usually write when they attend my seminars and are asked to express gratitude for something they want. But this is the wrong approach because every result depends on the occurrence of an external event for what they want. So let's look at the right way to practise gratitude.

Step 1: Count Your Blessings

Say thank you every morning when you open your eyes before you get up. Say thank you for your life, the air you breathe, the bed you slept in, the bathroom, the shower, the running water, the heating, the electricity, your beating heart, your healthy lungs, your toothpaste, your toothbrush; say thank you for everything you have taken for granted for years. Before you eat and drink, say 'thank you' and mean it.

Step 2: Do Not Criticise

Avoid criticising your family, friends, colleague and even strangers on the road. When you feel like criticising someone or something, silently say, "Thank you" and "I love you" until you feel peace and gratitude towards your friends, family, colleagues and the strangers that pass through your life.

Notice everything that is good about everyone you know. Remember that, like you, none of us is perfect. You will attract more criticism or more things for you to criticise if you focus on being negative. When you criticise, you give away your good and block your prosperity.

Step 3: Journal Every Day

Every night, before you go to bed, take out your journal and write down at least five things you are grateful for that day. Finish each sentence with thank you, thank you, thank you. Here are some examples from my journal:

1) With all my heart, thank you for the experience I had in Kenya with Homeless International.

2) The experience has opened my eyes to how blessed and fortunate I am. I am truly grateful. Thank you, thank you and thank you.

3) I am truly grateful for the telephone conversation I had with my sister in Singapore. I miss her and please keep her safe. Thank you, thank you and thank you.

4) I am truly grateful for the money to pay the school fees today. Thank you, thank you and thank you.

5) I am truly grateful for the nose clip that was given to Hannah from Tanya. Another gift from

6) The Universe. Thank you, thank you and thank you.

7) I am truly grateful for the chocolate cake that Roger baked today. Everyone enjoyed it.

Thank you, thank you, and thank you.

When you are feeling grateful, you will have peace and you will experience true happiness. When you are happy, you raise your vibrations so you attract people and events that have the same vibrations as you. Whether you are consciously aware of it or not, when you express gratitude, you will filtered out all the incompatible people and events from your life and replace them with compatible ones. This explains why old friends move on and new friends enter your life.

Practise gratitude every day and you will experience miracles in your life. Magic happens. Have faith and take inspired action. Follow your passion, live the life of your dreams.

Practise Receiving

There are three simple steps to creating and manifesting the life of your dreams:

1) Ask
2) Have faith and be patient
3) Receive

We are very good at asking. Once we ask, The Universe starts to prepare to deliver us what we want. But how ready are you to receive? Many times, we block what we want to manifest because we do not believe we are worthy of receiving what we asked for. The Universe delivers, "Knock, knock, special delivery!" But it's as if you are saying, "Nobody is home—go away!"

- When a friend offers to buy you a coffee, what do you say?
- When a colleague offers you a piece of cake, what do you say?
- When your neighbour buys you a loaf of bread, what do you say?

Do you say, "No, thank you. I am fine'? Why do you say "No"? These are gifts from The Universe, gifts from God? Don't be someone who says "No" to the gifts that come your way. If you are someone who feels uncomfortable about accepting gifts from life, you will never be ready to receive what you have asked of The Universe. Do you remember when I talked about Anchoring Your Prosperity? The same principle applies with accepting gifts. You must make a statement to The Universe that proves you are ready to receive. Show The Universe that you believe you deserve every gift it sends to you and that you will gracefully receive each one with joy and gratitude. When you show The Universe you are ready and now everything you asked for will come to you at the perfect time.

Practise Forgiveness

"When you hold resentment toward another, you are bound to that person or condition by an emotional link that is stronger than steel. Forgiveness is the only way to dissolve that link and get free."

CATHERINE PONDER

Practicing forgiveness will release blocks from your life for good. It will open the floodgates of prosperity and bring blessings to your life. In an earlier chapter, I talked about forgiveness and the impact it has on our emotions and thoughts. When we bear grudges, it effects our emotions and impacts on the level of our vibrations, whether we are aware of it or not. When we release low or negative vibrational thoughts and emotions, we attract events, people and situations with similar vibrations. In other words, we get more of what we focus on.

In 1903 James Allen wrote, "The remembering of injuries is spiritual darkness; the fostering of resentment is spiritual suicide. To resort to the spirit and practise of forgiveness is the beginning of enlightenment. It is also the beginning of peace and happiness."

It is important that you forgive everyone for your own good. It is not about doing well for those who have done you wrong. If you want to create a life of prosperity, good health and happiness, there is no other way but to release resentment and practise forgiveness. Here's how you can start:

1)   Write a letter to someone who has done wrong against you and tell them exactly how you feel. Release the anger, resentment, fear, anxiety or whatever emotion you are experiencing. Do not hold back; you are allowed to use any language you wish. Express your feelings as fully as you wish so they are released. Once you have finished, read it out loud standing in front of a mirror then burn the letter. While the letter is burning, say, "I release you from my life. I forgive you for everything. I have moved on."

2)   Here's a prayer by Catherine Ponder that you can say every night before you go to bed. It will help to release any emotions around

negative events that have taken place during the day. If there is someone you would like to forgive, hold the person in your mind and say this prayer slowly and quietly, with feelings:

All that has offended me, I forgive within and without. I forgive things past, things present, things future. I forgive. I forgive everything and everyone who can possibly need forgiveness in my past and present. I forgive positively everyone including myself. I am free and all others are free too. All things are cleared up between us, now and forever.

Try it, you will feel much lighter after you have released the resentment. You will feel free and at peace. Once you have forgiven and released the burden of your emotions, your vibration will rise, the darkness will lift and you will be in a position to receive all the good your heart desires. The floodgates of good health, prosperity, success and happiness will be open for you. All you have to do is be ready to receive. Woohoo!!

Understand the Power of Words

One of my best friends from my village, Ping, is a Methodist. During Chinese New Year, she came to my house for lunch. My mum and grandma had prepared a feast. There was sesame chicken, roast duck, roast pork, king prawns, fish as well as many vegetables and lettuce wraps. Ping sat looking at all the dishes but dared not move her chop-sticks while the rest of us dug in. My grandma asked her why she was not eating. She said that her mum had told her that she is not allowed to eat food which has been offered to the deities as it is against her Christian beliefs. My grandma said to her, "What goes into the mouth is not harmful, what comes out of the mouth can be poisonous, it can harm like a thousand knives."

My grandma didn't intend to criticise the Bible or its teachings, she was just merely stating her belief based on her life experiences. What she said is very true: words can be more dangerous than a thousand knives. Words can heal, love, hurt, empower, degrades, manipulate, encourage, excite and much more besides. Hannah went through a period once when she would say hurtful things in the heat of a moment. When this happened, I would always stop and ask, "Do you really mean what you just said?" So far, her answers have been in 'No.' But if you do not mean what you say, don't say it.

Words themselves do not have any power. The power lies in how the words make us feel. If you can ignore the words and pay no attention to what others say to you, then the words will have no power over you. Not many people can do that, though. So, we must watch what we say to people. We must not intentionally hurt or harm others with our words, in fact, we must not aim to hurt or harm at all.

Words have the power to generate strong emotions in us, so use words to encourage, empower, create hope and express love, excitement, joy, peace and happiness. Affirmations work because they are words that encourage, empower, excite and create positive emotions. Positive emotions create high-level vibrations, which will in turn attract into your life the events and people who are at a similar vibrational frequency.

Use your words carefully in everyday conversation. If you are having a 'bad day', don't go around telling everyone you meet. What can these people do? Can they improve your day? No, I can guarantee they can't because when you tell them the story of your 'bad day', you are focusing on the 'low-level vibrations'. The more you vibrate at a low frequency, more low frequency events and people will be attracted to you. It may not manifest on the same day, but it will manifest eventually; especially, if you have been focusing on it with energy. So instead of having one 'bad day', it may mean you end up having several 'bad days'. Do not feed negative energy, focus on positive energy.

Do not criticise, gossip, complain or listen to sad stories. How your friends behave is their choice, and you do not need to replicate it with everyone you meet by criticising their behaviour. If you disapprove of their behaviour, just make sure you do not join it or do it yourself. You cannot attract money if you criticise money at the same time. You cannot attract love if you complain about how much love hurts or get involved in your friend's divorce story. You cannot attract good grades at school whilst all the time complaining about how unfair the grading system is or how your teachers are biased or not very good. Remember to use words carefully and be aware of how they make you feel before saying them. Think about how your words will make others feel before you say them. If they make you feel uncomfortable, choose different words.

Never Give Up

Be persistent and never give up. Use the tools listed here that feel right for you and do not keep looking for the sign that they are working. Practise with faith, trusting that the Universe is working to deliver everything you ask for at the perfect time. God and the Universe are never late.

Go to this website, (www.samrayner.co.uk) to download the workbook and 30-day Manifestation Action Plan. Follow it for 30 days, and you will see changes in your life. Be persistent and be patient. Do not give up. The action plan will stand you in good stead for manifesting all your dreams for the future.

Dear Hannah,

This is the end of this book, so it's time for the curtain to come down. There may not be an encore, so I hope I have passed on some wisdom, a little bit of vulnerability, a dash of excitement, a handful of faith and an ocean full of love—my love for you.

Your life is a journey, a hero's journey. You are the creator of your life and the author of every story and adventure life can bring. I can assure you that there will not be sunshine every day, but it is guaranteed that rainbows follow every storm. It is in the storm that our personalities and characters are shaped. In the storm of life, we discover our courage and our strength.

The storms of life are the challenges we face throughout our journey. Challenges present themselves along the way at various points in our journey. Each challenge holds a lesson for us, with the intention of shaping our personality and character so it can prepare us for our next adventure. If we did not grasp the lesson in a particular challenge, the universe and God will continue to present similar situations until we finally 'get it'.

On that note, when faced with each challenge, do not charge at it like a bull in a china shop. Take a step back, look at the situation in front of you and learn the lesson it is presenting to you. Once you see the lesson, you will come up with the perfect solution. Have courage that you can face each challenge with poise and calm and trust that the best solution will always be presented to you when you have a calm and quiet mind.

Live your life with passion, love and compassion. Never aim to change anyone but yourself. Accept and love people just as they are. More importantly, accept and love yourself just as you are, know and believe that you are SPECIAL and never let anyone tell you otherwise.

Never commit to marriage if you feel you will have to put up with traits or habits you can't endure. Don't for one minute think you can change him. Leave immediately and do not look back because your perfect match is standing at the next crossroads waiting for you!

I love you, Hannah. Be happy.

"Courage is not the absence of fear, but rather the judgement that something else is more important than fear."

James Neil Hollingsworth

Have Faith in God, Trust in the Universe, Have Courage to Take Action, Live Your Passion.

Always with you, Mummy

LIST OF BOOKS FOR FURTHER READING

- *Manifesting Change* by Mike Dooley
- *Leveraging the Universe* by Mike Dooley
- *Miracle Morning* by Hal Elrod
- *Abundance Now* by Lisa Nichols
- *Breaking the Habit of Being Yourself* by Dr Joe Dispenza
- *You Are the Placebo* by Dr Joe Dispenza
- *Mind Over Medicine* by Dr Lisa Rankin
- *Wishes Fulfilled* by Dr Wayne W. Dyer
- *Ordering from The Cosmic Kitchen* by Patricia J. Crane, Ph.D

GUIDE TO CHINESE FAMILY NAMES

Tai Poh	Great Grandma (mother's side)
Tai Mah	Great Grandma (father's side)
Gong-Gong	Grandpa
Poh-Poh	Grandma
Kao Fu	Uncles
YI-Yi	Aunts
Yi Gu Ma	Second aunt from father's side (my father's younger sister); Yi means second child; Gu Ma means aunt from father's side

ABOUT THE AUTHOR

Phui Yee has been working as a Building Surveyor and Project Manager for the past 18 years. As part of her work, she meets both adults and children who live in poverty and suffer financial hardship. She has always wondered how she can help these people improve their life and help them see there is another way.

No answers were given until six years ago when Phui Yee's life was turned upside down. Her yellow brick road crumbled before her eyes. It was in this darkest moment of her life that she found the answer to her question and a way not only to help herself to rebuild her life and given her the skills and knowledge to help others as well.

It is Phui Yee's passion to reach out to as many people as she can around the world so she can help to create a prosperous future for all who are willing to walk the path with her.